Building a Kindness Army

The Passionate Fight against Food Insecurity

Katie Dahlheim

Founder, Lowcountry Blessing Box Project

i

Building a Kindness Army

Cover design and artwork: Kayla Boyter

LCCN: 2021910438

ISBN 978-0-578-92019-1 (paperback)

ISBN XXX-X-XXXXX-XXX-X (e-book)

Printed in the United States of America

www.twitter.com/chsblessingbox

www.facebook.com/chsblessingbox

For Claire and Quinn

Chapter 1: Building a Kindness Army

There is an army of kind people in Charleston, South Carolina. It has always been here, but it took a few years of organizing to manifest itself into more than 200 small wooden boxes scattered over the area as a visible sign of its existence.

In 2017, I was searching for something that could bring everyone together. Charleston had been through several local tragedies in the preceding years, and following the 2016 election, the political climate of the country was more turbulent than I had ever experienced.

Eventually, it occurred to me that it is as simple as this: we can all afford to be kinder to one another. Kinder in our words, kinder in our thoughts, and kinder in our deeds. It needn't matter if you're a red-stater or a blue-stater, anonymous giving is the perfect vessel for slow but impactful change. An army of people who are determined to increase the values of empathy and tolerance is the catalyst we need to slowly, methodically fight back against the divisiveness in our local communities and beyond.

With this guiding principle in mind, I created the Lowcountry Blessing Box Project, and its rapid growth and popularity has inspired others not only to participate by anonymously donating food but also to contribute in many other ways. The Blessing Box Project is a network of anonymous food donation sites with one guideline: leave what you can, take what you need. I have been rewarded ten times over by the people who have joined me in this Kindness Army. I have made friends and important connections, but it has been so much more for me as well.

Raised to Serve

I grew up as a Catholic school kid. Each month our class had an organized service project, and because of these monthly projects, I was inspired early on to make a difference for people who were situated differently from me. I distinctly remember tearing apart my mom's couch looking for discarded change to add to my little "Trick-or-Treat for UNICEF" milk carton because we had been given a handout that said just a few cents could feed a hungry child in a third-world country. Moreover, I understood that if a few cents could feed one child, then a few dollars could feed a dozen. I never grew out of this drive to help others.

As a young adult, I was drawn to law school because of the opportunities to make change that come with being an attorney and my continuing motivation to be a "helper." I would be oversimplifying if I told you I had a specific career plan and that everything turned out as I imagined it would when I sat for the LSAT at age twenty-one. In college, I had aspirations of working in child advocacy that emerged while I was employed at a children's group home, and I chose my law school based on its work on adoption law and policy. However, it is funny where life takes you, and in all my years of practice I have never helped anyone adopt a child. Upon passing the bar, my first job was as a public defender. If you had asked me in law school what kind of law I wanted to practice, being a public defender would have been very far down on my list.

Luckily, I had some great mentors and coworkers early in my career who helped me understand the role of a public defender in the judicial system, and how to zealously advocate for my clients. I learned that my natural inclination to empathize with someone's situation was often an asset in my job because it helped me tell their story, whether that was to a jury during a trial or to a judge who would be passing a sentence. Telling someone's story and painting the picture of how they came to be standing before the court that

2

day was a part of the practice of law that I did not know existed until I did it, but also the part I probably excelled at the most.

It was not until well into my adult life that I realized not everyone has the same bend toward empathy that I first felt as a child. Upon that realization, though, I came to understand that in order to motivate someone to help others, they might need to understand why the person needs help in the first place. In other words, the anonymous giving I had set out to inspire by creating the Blessing Box Project would not happen without some level of imagination. When our donors give, I think they each have their own imagined person in mind who will be assisted by their donations. To some it might be a single parent, to others a senior citizen, to others a person who might not have a home, and still to others, a person like them but after a few bad months of unexpected expenses or bad luck. This image, created in each donor's mind, is what keeps them coming back with their canned goods.

My Project is and always has been about more than just food. It is about building community, encouraging kindness, and teaching each other about empathy. I hope that every time you see a Blessing Box or a Little Free Pantry in your neighborhood, you will know that no matter how terrible the world gets, how bleak your situation seems, or how lonely the days are—someone out there cares about you and believes that we will get through things together.

Chapter 2: Ya'll Wanna See the Hawgs?

"Ya'll wanna see the hawgs?" asked John, an adorable barefoot four-year-old boy. This was my first official welcome to Whitesville, West Virginia, in the summer of 1999. John was the youngest of the family of six my group had come to help. During our five-day trip to the hills of Appalachia, we built a three-room addition to John's family's trailer. The purpose of this trip was not to evangelize, but it was my introduction to seeing my religion in practice. It opened my eyes to see that not just adults, but kids too, can make real, tangible change when we leave our comfort zones. This trip would also lead me to form my first nonprofit organization.

Lending a Hand

Our trip began on a Thursday in late July. It was hot and nineteen of us—mostly teenagers and a few college chaperones—had loaded our bags into four vehicles and driven six hours into the hills of Appalachia, arriving just before midnight. We stayed at the charming Bed & Barn, a quaint house with several cats, pickup trucks littering the lawn, and coal miners staying in the other rented rooms. We slept on the floor, and the college kids who drove us down woke us the first day by blasting "Good Morning, Vietnam" at 0600 hours.

The first morning we met the foreman, who, as a result of a hunting accident "gone bad," had one missing thumb, a glass eye, and several missing teeth. Fortunately for those of us under his direction, he was also blessed with an extraordinary amount of patience, a wonderful heart, and an unforgettable sense of humor. Over the workdays ahead, he explained what we were to do as many times as we required and then yelled, "Aight?" By the end of the first day, we teenagers were yelling "Aight!" right back at him in our best Southern West Virginia accents.

The heat index in the mountains of West Virginia is not quite as harsh as it is in my adoptive hometown of Charleston, South Carolina, but at the time it felt like we were standing on the sun. Despite the miserable weather, though, we had removed a wall from a family's home, and we weren't leaving until they had three more bedrooms in their impossibly crammed trailer. While cooling off in the creek next to the house, I began to understand the privilege of my upbringing, and I also started to acknowledge the desire to give back that would live in my heart for years to come.

On our last workday in Whitesville, the weather was hot, and tempers were growing hotter as we realized some of our work on the roof was incorrect and would need to be completely removed and redone. Balanced on a board twelve feet off the ground while hammering nails is not my preferred scenario for a heart-to-heart conversation, but that was precisely the situation that had presented itself. John's father, who owned the trailer, was working alongside us. He was my partner for our section of the roof, and he told me about his work in a local factory where he hung sheets of steel. He worked hard to support his family and was humbled to require the assistance of teenagers. I could feel his gratitude, even without him having to put it specifically into words. I empathized with how an adult must feel to need the help of volunteers to house his family. We ended up coming back to John's house again the following summer to hang drywall, paint, and reroute the creek so that the newly finished house would be safe from flooding.

Forming an Official Nonprofit

After nine years of making trips to the Southern Coal Fields region of West Virginia, my friends and I decided that our disorganized, money-in-a-coffee-can, thrown-together trips to Appalachia could be something more. At that time, I had finished my first year of law school, and I submitted our application to be recognized as an official nonprofit organization by the IRS. It was called Lend-a-Hand for Appalachia.

Legitimizing an effort like Lend-a-Hand served a few purposes. First, by becoming a nonprofit organization, monetary donations from supporters could be tax deductible. When we were throwing the cash from car wash fundraisers into a box and hoping to have enough for gas money to Southern West Virginia, we were always grateful, but we were not able to offer that tax benefit to our donors. Other reasons to become exempt included some state and local tax benefits, eligibility to apply for grants, establishment of a formal structure that we could put on our resumes, and limiting the liability of our founders, directors, and members (we are talking about hormonal teenagers with power tools here!).

Organizations of do-gooders can exist and fully function in their communities without applying for tax-exempt, nonprofit status, and in many cases, it is not a necessary step. It requires a startup cost, paperwork, and commitment, and sometimes these hurdles may not be worth the effort. An organization's founders must also consider loss of control—when you have a board of directors, which many states require for nonprofits, then the decision-making shifts from the folks who thought up the mission to the people sitting on the board. A nonprofit organization is subject to laws and regulations, including its own articles of incorporation and bylaws, whereas a group of friends doing some good deeds is not. Also, a nonprofit, because it is dedicated to the public interest, will have to open its books to be inspected by the public.

With all these considerations, consultation with a knowledgeable attorney or accountant before forming a nonprofit is well worth the expense. I still hold a tiny grudge against my law school professor who would not help me with the IRS application fifteen years ago. Luckily, the process has become less arduous since the first time I went through it.

Lend-a-Hand for Appalachia still exists today—and more than twenty years' worth of high school classes have made similar trips, met similar folks, and completed similar projects. The trips we planned always followed the same format, with time for group reflection at the end. We talked to the students about the necessity of leaving our comfort zones to understand and empathize with others, and we discussed the importance of putting religious faith into practice.

The most important lesson I learned in the coalfields of West Virginia was that until we put the teachings from church and our religion classes at school into action, there would be no real change.

Chapter 3: Formation of the Blessing Box Project

In the late fall of 2016, I started following dozens of Black women on Twitter. I came to understand that while many people were surprised by the results of the 2016 presidential election, lots of Black women were not. They read the tea leaves I did not even know to look for—and theirs was a perspective I needed in my daily scrolling on the internet. As the country felt fractured more each day, I began wondering how ordinary people like me could bridge a gap or channel the energy that had been rising in many of us as we wondered what would become of our society. What could everyone agree on? What was not "political"? What could possibly unify us?

Like most parents of small children, I do my best thinking in the shower—that is, when I get a whole shower with no interruptions, no audience members, and no requests to "just watch what I can do!" I considered the need for a homeless shelter for LGBTQ teens who had been turned out by their families. One of my closest confidants reminded me to stay in my lane, and my lane did not include being a savior for LGBTQ youth, so back to the shower musings I went. As the turmoil that followed the election rolled on, I had a recurring thought—"This is not who we are. Who will bring us back together?"

In 2017, everything felt very splintered, divided, contentious. It was naïve of me to think that this was new—this country has been divided in many ways since its creation, but for the first time in my adult life I was more acutely aware of the separations and daily disagreements happening around me. The privilege of being born a straight, white woman largely had insulated me from that reality up to that point. I really wanted to find something that I felt everyone could agree on, no matter who they were, where they were from, what they believed, or whether they were on team red or team blue. Eventually, I surmised that maybe everyone can agree that we should just be kinder to each other. To me, kindness often translates into being nonjudgmental of others.

Being nicer to people may seem like a simple, even childlike idea, but it is also a noble one. Here in Charleston, South Carolina, several events unfolded in the years leading up to 2017 that were very fracturing for the community, particularly the tragedy at Mother Emanuel AME Church where a white supremacist murdered nine Black worshipers. There was also a police shooting of an unarmed Black man during a traffic stop—and both events happened within one month of each other. It was and still is difficult for our community to reckon with these tragedies. But in our shared state of disheartenment and discord, the idea of anonymous giving seemed promising as a tiny path forward. What if we could just all put everything aside and give to someone without having to interact with them? There would be no judgment, no discussion. They wouldn't have to say thank you or explain why they needed it, and you wouldn't know who got it.[1] What if we just started doing things to make a stranger's day better? What if there was a very simple way to put kindness into the world that people could participate in on their own terms and at their convenience?

---

[1] This is not to say that we can heal our deep wounds without interacting with one another – quite the opposite is true. We must, as Bernice King instructed on her visit to Charleston following the tragedies in 2015, get to know one another on deeper levels. We must eat dinner with people who do not look like us or share our background.

Learn more about an organization leading that charge, Transformation Table, at www.transformationtable.com.

The Birth of the Blessing Box

Around that time, I read about Jessica McClard in Arkansas, who created a Little Free Pantry at her home.[2] A Little Free Pantry is an anonymous food donation site located in a place that is always publicly accessible. This concept seemed like something we all could get behind: everyone needs to eat. My half-Italian heart was overjoyed with this realization and the idea of feeding lots of people. My brain was set into motion. My lane-secure confidant assured me that anonymously feeding people was an appropriate avenue to explore.

I searched the web for more pantries and found one person in Oklahoma who was calling hers a "Blessing Box." I do like alliteration. And I live in the South, where we love to "bless" things—your heart, your day. A plan was coming together—I would make free pantries and call them Blessing Boxes. But where would I put them, and would anyone even care? I live on a cul-de-sac, so no one was going to happen to be passing by my house to see a pantry in my front yard. At this point I did what all logical people do—I decided if I couldn't have one, then I would have a dozen, and I would do this with the help of strangers from the internet.

To put my plan in motion, I decided to build a few pantries myself with the intention of giving them away to people who worked, lived, or worshiped in high-traffic and/or underserved areas. By the end of March 2017, I had obtained three old kitchen cabinets from a secondhand store and another from my friend's barn. I used these to build the first four Blessing Boxes in my garage. It was imperative that they had plexiglass fronts so people could see that there was food inside, and I decided that no one ever disliked a matching color scheme, so I painted them all red and blue. Was that subconsciously patriotic? Maybe. It could also be that the only

---

[2] Learn more about Little Free Pantry at www.littlefreepantry.org.

exterior paint in stock at my local store that day was Barnhouse Red, and we happened to have some blue in the garage. My budget at this point was zero, and my husband may or may not have been questioning my sanity. Bless his heart.

I have a friend who works in construction and asked him to come over for a consultation on how to weatherproof the indoor cabinets I had obtained. We spent about two hours trying to cut the doors to make a place for plexiglass, during which time one of our tiniest participants spilled red paint all over the garage floor. The period of trial and error began. I decided I would use extra shingles we had left over from updating our shed to cover the roofs of my four would-be Blessing Boxes. Shoutout to those who helped me acquire roofing skills as a volunteer in the hills of West Virginia. It was a long day full of challenges, but by the end, we had a general prototype and a plan.

After a few more weeks of work, I had four Boxes ready to go and had ordered bumper stickers with the words "Leave what you can, Take what you need." I moved on to the next phase of my plan. I gave the Boxes away to people I connected with on Facebook furniture swap sites. This served three purposes: (1) I could start publicizing the idea of a free pantry network online, (2) I could look for more unused cabinets that might be donated to my effort, and most importantly, (3) I could find more "hosts" and maybe even donors who wanted to get involved in my mission. At this same time, unbeknownst to me, my dear friend had also built and installed a Little Free Pantry for her home. Thus, within a few weeks the first five Blessing Boxes were up and running!

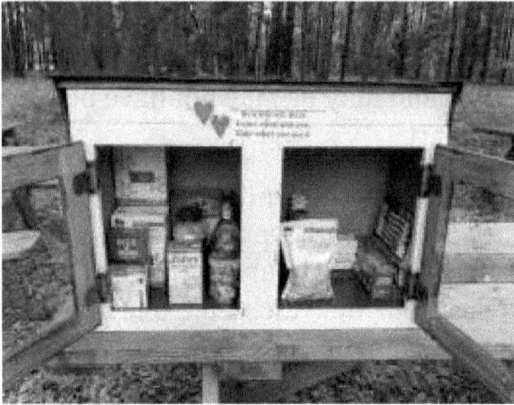

A Bumpy but Successful Launch

This launch was not without its problems. One of the Boxes ended up sitting out in the rain for so long that it was not usable by the time our host was ready to install it. Another was vandalized almost immediately. Others kept falling over—or were knocked over—and we had to keep picking them up and cleaning up all the food that had scattered during the fall. But I was steadfast in my plan. The first locations had been selected after much consideration, and for my plan to work, we had to just keep picking them up—literally—and cleaning them up until the community and its teenage vandals accepted they were here to stay.

These first placements were important. They had to be close to people who needed help. They had to have some shade and a space for donors or recipients to safely pull a vehicle off the road to restock or shop. They had to be spread out from one another but also convenient enough for either me or their designated host to check them frequently. At the time I was traveling the Lowcountry for work, with nine set destinations each month, so my original idea was that if I could place one Box near each of my work locations, I'd have a tiny network of pantries covering most of the greater Charleston area.

Thanks to significant local news coverage and social media, the word about the Lowcountry Blessing Box Project spread quickly. People were actually donating food, and someone was actually coming to get it—and not just occasionally, but every single day. The Project began growing steadily, with volunteers coming forward to host and build Boxes across the area. A real estate company was willing to be a host, and a community member stepped up to build a Blessing Box out of a jewelry cabinet. A senior center thought hosting a Box would be a great way to help their members on fixed incomes. A group of ladies running a summer camp decided to make one with their students. A Girl Scout troop planned to put one at a hair salon near my house.

Anonymous giving of nonperishable foods for anyone who wanted it, anytime day or night—no questions asked. This was something everyone could agree on—and this was the way we would start to spread kindness.

Chapter 4: Community Construction Day

In the heat of summer 2017, a plumber reached out to say he loved what I had created, and he wanted to make a monetary donation to create more Boxes. I told him that it was not an official organization and that he would have to just write the check to me personally. The Blessing Box Project did not even have a bank account.

He did not hesitate. He donated $500 by dropping it off at my office—we never even met in person. I think about him often, the plumber who did not want his name to be known but whom I will never forget. He changed my life. He took my Project from a little idea to a big deal. I never heard from him again, but I hope he has followed our growth. I hope he knows about the fire he lit and the development he spurred.

This gift of $500 felt like a huge investment at the time. I had spent about $100 of my own money and many hours, but this was someone else's money, and that someone believed in this mission. I decided to use that money to host a construction day, where we would build more Blessing Boxes. This idea naturally raised some questions. Should I invite volunteers to come to our house to construct them? If not, what kind of venue would even consider something like this—with the liability of untrained volunteers using power tools? After my experiences in West Virginia, the thought of those dangers threw the lawyer part of my brain into a tailspin.

Around the time I received the donation, I had been driving by a lovely green space on my way to work each morning. A former housing project, it was slowly being turned into an open area for community events. I decided to reach out to the owners—I wanted to use the space to host a construction day, but I also wanted to give them a Blessing Box for their property.

As the fates would have it, the folks at the site were open to my ideas and agreed to let us use their riverfront property to build our new Boxes. They would, however, require us to have our own insurance policy and incorporate as a legal entity. I expected this, but I had been putting it off because I already had a full plate with my full-time job, two kids, and other responsibilities. This was the push I needed, though, so our IRS application for nonprofit status, our bank account, and our insurance policy quickly came into existence. Within a few days, I created a letterhead and a liability waiver, formed a board of directors, and finalized a logo. Then I planned a construction day for June 4th, my parents' wedding anniversary. I did not think it hurt for the date to have some personal significance as I attempted to catapult my little Project into something more widespread and effective.

The Building Process

We had about two dozen volunteers in and out throughout the day. Two of them I gave birth to, and one I married. The rest were mostly friends, but about ten of them had read about what we were doing and saw the Facebook event page I had created. New blood!

We made the construction day Boxes from scratch according to a specific plan, using treated lumber, exterior screws, and exterior paint. They were tall and thin and painted red because, again, that was the only exterior paint color the hardware store nearest the site carried that day. They would withstand a hurricane, my friend who works in construction promised hopefully. This turned out to be true—we have had at least one named storm a year since 2017, and all the construction day Boxes are still going strong!

We scrapped our original building plans early in the day because we realized that if we made the Boxes skinnier, we could make an extra one with the donated plywood. I have building plans on our website that I have linked from the Little Free Pantry website, but to this day, none of the Boxes I've made have followed those particular plans.

The group worked hard building and painting, and at the end of the day, we had eight new Blessing Boxes ready to be placed around the Lowcountry.

After construction day, I realized that there were many willing hosts who lacked either the skills or resources, or both, to create their own Blessing Boxes. Creating a wooden box can seem an impossible task if you do not know where to begin. I also realized that others who enjoy building would consider it an easy weekend project. Part of my effort became connecting these two types of people. I did this by creating an online community as a Facebook Group page, which began with only local members but has grown since. People love to discuss the pros and cons, the lessons learned, and the pitfalls of building projects such as this, and I was able to give them that place to connect with each other.

Initial Tips and Expectations

As with any nice, new thing that is left out for anyone to access, vandalism will occur. It is almost always bored kids in the neighborhood, and it goes away on its own. We have had Boxes hit and knocked over, which we've picked up and reinstalled, and we have had many instances of someone dumping the contents of all the food packages from the Box onto the ground and leaving all the trash behind. If we worried for too long about any of these instances, we would probably start feeling discouraged, so each time we have just cleaned up the mess and carried on with the mission.

We have also had problems with the Box construction. Not all Blessing Boxes are built to withstand a storm—some are upcycled newspaper dispensers or kitchen cabinets. One is a bookshelf, and another is a DVD holder. We even had one made from a jewelry box, but admittedly, it didn't last very long.

Here are some more construction and maintenance tips to consider if you are thinking about building your own pantry:

- Use treated lumber and exterior paint. Bonus points for exterior artwork.
- Slant the roof so the rain runs off.
- Place the pantry in the shade, especially if you are in the South, because a closed box in the sun can get hot enough to warp some types of packaging.
- It should be located where someone will check on it several times a week, if not daily, to get rid of any bugs and trash.
- Encourage your community to be involved in the general upkeep and cleanliness of the pantry. This is, after all, a community project. The goal is not to have one person monitoring and cleaning it; we want everyone to feel responsible for doing that. We want everyone to understand that if they go to the Blessing Box and there are ants in it or something has spilled, they should clean that up. If there's trash in it, they should throw it away.
- Mount the Box on a 4x4 post off the ground to help keep animals out and cement it down.
- Make sure the door securely closes and latches.
- Ideally, the front should be see-through, either glass or plexiglass, so when you drive or walk by, you will know if

something is inside. Plexiglass is much cheaper, and most hardware stores will cut it to size for you.

- The Box should be easily identifiable as a food pantry, not a site for books or clothes, by either decals or painting.
- If you are able, place a solar light on the Box for shoppers, donors, and passersby who might otherwise assume something suspicious is going on at night.
- Many of our Boxes have small baskets inside to hold toiletries or other nonfood donations like socks since those are necessities as well.
- If you don't want to do the construction yourself, think about other community groups that might be able to assist you. Are there youth groups at your church? Are your grandkids in scouts? Does your local high school teach a shop class?

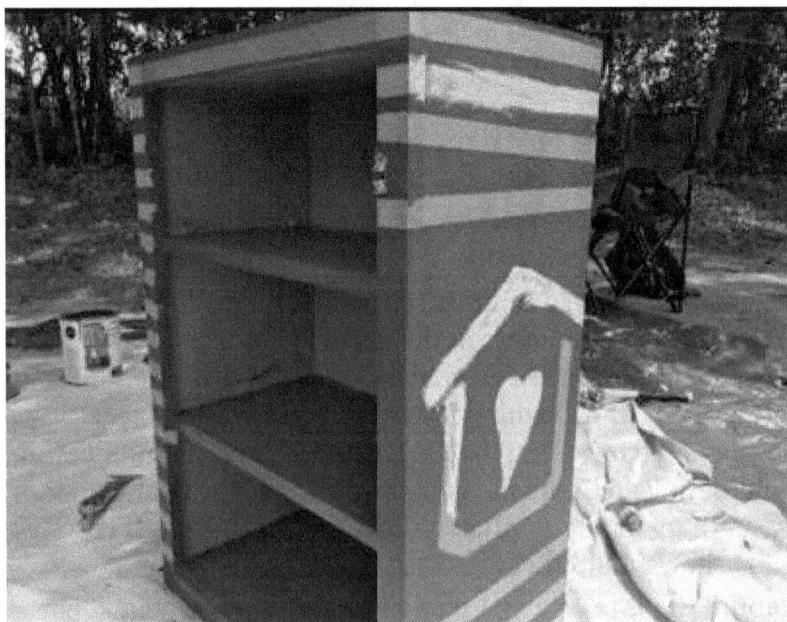

We have applied for only one grant in our four years of existence, and it was to put solar lighting on many of our Blessing Boxes. We had an incident where a person was at a Box at night, and a car came by whose driver shone their bright lights on him to confront him about what he was doing. Maybe they thought he was stealing—or perhaps they knew the purpose of the Box and wanted to embarrass him. Regardless, it was traumatic for him. After this incident, we added solar lights to that location and several more Boxes to help not only the recipient who might feel uncomfortable coming during the day, but also people who do not know the purpose of the Box. With the solar lights, you can tell that the structure is intentionally there and somebody is not just doing something trifling in the dark.

Several of our pantries are made from newspaper dispensers that our local paper was willing to donate. A few adjustments can disable the locking mechanism so that money is not required to open them, and they are ready to be out on the streets quickly. One of our most loyal volunteers secured this donation for us. He passed away during the coronavirus pandemic, and his daughter called me to tell me the news. She said her mother mentioned that they should break the news to me—on the same day he passed, just like I was family.

My heart melted. It told me what the Project meant to him— that he talked about it at home with his loved ones often and that they had embraced it too. Although he and I were of different generations, with different upbringings and different political perspectives, this simple idea that we should be kinder to one another united us.

Chapter 5: Creating a Network of Blessing Boxes

Following construction day, strangers routinely started contacting me about building their own Boxes, and churches with existing pantries reached out to be added to our list. The mayor's office ran a summer camp for area youth to do service projects, and they built a Blessing Box out of an old DVD stand. It was covered in the kids' handprints and quotes about kindness. They placed it inside a laundromat, which at the time was our only Blessing Box located inside a business, the majority of them being outdoors so they are available anytime, day or night.[1]

The Blessing Box at the laundromat has long been a favorite of mine because it was created by kids, and those kids now know that they can change our city—their city—by their small act of kindness. We have a standing monthly online order to deliver food and laundry supplies to that Box because it's used so frequently. I think this is a great use of the monetary donations we receive. Also, that particular Blessing Box has led to an ongoing partnership with the laundromat that evolved into us hosting free laundry events at their site.

Today, there are more than two hundred existing sites with Blessing Boxes in the South Carolina Lowcountry. After the initial dozen—the four from my garage and the eight from construction day—I have not picked up a hammer. My tools of choice have instead been my iPhone and my voice. I have spoken at churches, luncheons, universities, ladies' nights, and many other events to

---

[1] We now have another indoor Blessing Box, at a secondhand furniture store that operates in support of another nonprofit. The rest of the Boxes in our network remain accessible 24/7.

spread our mission and our message. I have done countless media interviews, appearances on internet talk shows, and podcasts.[2]

Perhaps most importantly, I created and maintain social media accounts to keep people engaged and inspired to continue their anonymous giving. Within a year of our first Box going up, the following on our social media accounts was well into the thousands, and our network of Blessing Boxes had grown to around forty places to "leave what you can or take what you need."

The explosion of growth forced me to give up my tightly held plan regarding the placement of the Boxes. I encourage anyone who asks—and they don't all ask—to check our constantly changing Google Map of locations to make sure they are not about to place a Box right next to an existing one. If there is more than one pantry in the area, then the donations will be spread out over the two locations instead of centralized in one place. Someone would have to know—and have the means—to visit both of them to check for food.

This idea of competing pantries is a challenge of anonymous giving—I have no idea whether this scenario happens in real life, but it makes sense in my head, and I don't have any data to prove or disprove my theory. If someone has set their mind to place a Box somewhere, I have not always been successful in convincing them to move it or to just contribute to the existing Box nearby. But I chalk

---

[2] My boss at the time was kind enough to let me roll with this idea of creating a network of free pantries without much pushback, despite our work in local government with politicians from a variety of backgrounds. In the beginning, I would let him know that I was doing an interview or going to be on TV, but these appearances quickly became so frequent that I stopped telling him every time, and he stopped asking. I took this as a sign that my quest to create change without touching on a political hot-button issue had been fulfilled.

this up to a growing pain and move on. In the end, people are donating, people are eating, and that's all that matters.

My desire has been and remains to inspire other people to do what needs to be done in their community, as opposed to micromanaging and being in control of exactly what's happening at each location. Other organizations have seen what we are doing and replicated it in some manner, giving no credit to us or to the original Little Free Pantry in Arkansas. If someone is inspired by what we do and wants to put their own spin on it, that is great. I hope they have an impact and help people. That is, after all, the ultimate goal.

I have tried hard not to put my face on this Project because, by definition, it should be faceless. However, the world and social media do not always function that way, and someone has to make the contacts, give the interviews, and spread the message.

I follow several other free pantry hosts on social media, and I see lots of videos of hosts daily narrating what is in the pantry, explaining what it needs, and thanking those who have donated for the week by name. I have purposefully chosen not to center the Project around any one person or group of volunteers because I think anonymity is the beauty of the Project. The focus must be on the mission, not the people. It doesn't matter why you're giving or taking food—everybody is in this journey of life together. Let's strive to make each other's trips more pleasant.

Tips for Creating a Successful Pantry Network

The idea of an interconnected network of food donation locations is catching on nationwide, and most recently I have been seeing the same concept with refrigerators, or "Free Fridges." Our network originated because I live on a cul-de-sac and did not think placing a Blessing Box at my own house would be effective. While I had no idea how popular my idea would become, I am so grateful that it has been embraced.

Part of the Project's success is simply because of how easy it is for both participants and recipients. These days, everyone thinks of themselves as the busiest person they know—it's like a badge of honor to be busy. In order to make this Project successful, I knew it had to be easy. No forms, no lists, no keeping track of items or scheduling drop-offs. And for those shopping at the Boxes, it had to be a completely judgment-free experience. No one wants to explain to a stranger, or worse, a friend, why they need to get macaroni and cheese out of a box on the side of a street on a weeknight or else their kids won't have dinner.

Aside from generally keeping things simple, here are some specific tips for successfully creating a network of Boxes:

- If you are going to make more than one Box, coordinate the colors and decals to create a brand. This is especially important if you are also making a social media account or website to promote your pantry network. The size and shape of the structures themselves matters less than uniting them with either a color scheme or matching decals.

- Create an easily accessible way for people to navigate between your locations—like a Google Map or another app with mapping capabilities. This is especially important as your project grows because you don't want someone to give up when they find an empty Box if there could be a full one very nearby.

- Do your research first and make sure you are not violating any local ordinances or laws. Some localities outlaw giving away food without permits or require approval from the health department. It is better to know your rules before you begin.[3]

- Don't require design standards. We don't have any regulations or thoughts on appearance—your Blessing Box can be any size, shape, or color to be included in our network. It can be huge or tiny; it can have purple polka dots or match the red-and-blue color scheme that many of our Boxes use. I think when you limit someone's creativity or place requirements on a design, it discourages participation.

- Require the landowner's permission to place Boxes. We require people to affirm that they have gotten permission from whoever owns the land—often that's the host themselves, but it could be a landlord. If it's a church or other house of worship, then it needs to be the governing body. I learned this the hard way when a tenant who had been a host moved out, and the landlord contacted me angrily asking about the wooden box on his lawn.

- Include updated Box locations on your website. Once the host has permission and has built and installed the Box, they send me a picture along with the location's address so I can add it to the map, to the list on our website, and on social media. If they request it, I will send decals with our logo and the words "Leave what you can, Take what you need." I also used to provide a metal plate printed with a legal disclaimer, but as our network grew and grew, it became too expensive. Instead, I now provide the new hosts with the wording and tell them they can print and laminate it to post on their Box.

---

[3] Do not assume that because you have seen other pantries that it is legal where you are. Do thorough research on your own, or contact a local lawyer for help.

- Understand that you will not have control of the Boxes you do not own, did not build, or did not coordinate to create. If the organization that hosts the Box wants to use it to include religious literature, that is probably not something you can control. If they want to put a video camera on the Box to see who is taking things, you probably do not have the right to ask them to take it down. The Lowcountry Blessing Box Project as an organization has become more of a clearinghouse for information than anything else; we have not had a hand in building or placing the Boxes in several years. Now the focus of our mission is more on helping people find information about the locations, the purpose, what to donate, and other important tips than on creating the Boxes themselves.

- Keep the hosts in the loop. We send out a monthly newsletter to tell folks if any Boxes have come down and where new locations have been installed within the past month. We use it as a way to keep in touch with our donors and to incorporate a theme when appropriate, like back-to-school supply donations, Thanksgiving meal bags, or dental hygiene month toiletries. The newsletter also highlights upcoming events we may be running with some of our community partners, like free laundry days or coat drives.

- Seek funding assistance. Organizations exist and give grants to build Blessing Boxes or Little Free Pantries. No Child Goes Hungry[4] is one such source of funding, and there are others.

- Ensure your Boxes are easy to find. We made a QR code that will pop up our map, website, and social media accounts. We use the QR code on our canvas banner that we take to events

---

[4] Learn more about No Child Goes Hungry at www.nochildgoeshungry.net/grants-in-motion/.

and on our business cards, which we place in the Boxes periodically. The trick with having so many locations is that they seem to be everywhere until the recipient is hungry and comes upon an empty one. We want to make it easy to find the next closest one in that situation.

- Partner with a local printing company that makes merchandise with your logo (ours does T-shirts, coffee mugs, tote bags, etc.) and donates a portion of each sale back to your organization.[5]

- Make an Amazon Wish List to publicize on your website and in your newsletter to allow folks to donate from the comfort of their couch. The items on our Wish List ship to one of our locations that has both a traditional Blessing Box for nonperishables and also a Free Community Fridge because it is centrally located in our city and has a very active and reliable host.

---

[5] You can shop our merchandise here: https://app.printyourcause.com/campaigns/LowcountryBlessingBox.

Above all else, here is the most important advice I have—just start. Start where you are. Start with whatever seems like the most logical step for you. The easiest way to figure out what is going to work in your community is to take the first steps and then adjust as needed. Maybe that means you put up a card table in your driveway, throw some groceries on it, and make a sign that tells people to take what they want.

Organic Growth

I never would have imagined that I would be the catalyst behind two-hundred-plus different donations sites, or that thousands of people would care what we are doing and follow us on social media. Initially, I thought a dozen sites would be cool for a small group of pantries, but my community's demand was much higher. I try to think of it this way: the community is steering the bike, and I am just here to pedal. Meaning, I may be the force behind the idea of anonymous giving and the expansion of the movement, but the community itself is now deciding where the Boxes will be placed and encouraging others to stock them. It is all happening organically.

JUNE 2017

June 2019

I have helped start both the Midlands Blessing Box Project and the Upstate Blessing Box Project here in South Carolina. Each has its own unique story of how it came to be—but now, along with a group that operates in the Pee Dee region, we are covering the entire state in opportunities for anonymous giving!

I also inspired my sister to begin a Blessing Box Project in her city in the Midwest. Her response has been much different from mine, and I think it is so interesting how a different region of the country has created a varying slant on the idea of a free pantry network.

My sister has had all kinds of problems that we never had. Some of the reasons behind these may be cultural, and some may be a matter of socioeconomics. Where we immediately had support from strangers on social media and had all our requests for donations fulfilled, she struggled. One Blessing Box host quit and took the Box down because she didn't like that people kept telling her to "have a blessed day."

Another host was cooking meals and putting them in the Boxes without understanding that the food must be nonperishable. The cook insisted on feeding the kids but couldn't appreciate the health risks. In the end, that Box had to be taken down as well. Despite these setbacks, she persisted and created a successful network of dozens of Blessing Boxes in her city.

Despite the possible geographic and cultural differences, I do believe that anonymous giving crosses into nearly all religions, and that our success is largely based on the idea that no matter what ideological beliefs we hold, helping others should be universal. Our Blessing Boxes are at Baptist churches, Catholic churches, AME churches, and mosques. One young man used his bar mitzvah to create bags full of food to donate in our Boxes. A host in my sister's project is a self-described Satanist. Kindness is for everyone.

Chapter 6: Exponential Growth

Some months our growth was incremental—and other times explosive. I found that interviews, even those broadcasted on the evening news or as headlines in our local paper, did not directly increase our social media following as much as viral content on our accounts. However, the number of likes on an internet post does not always translate into action. It takes a multitude of approaches to build a coalition.

A church organized "Charleston Love Week" where their volunteers built five more Blessing Boxes and found homes for all of them. A global corporation with local offices built a Blessing Box and spread the word to their five thousand employees around the world. Very often, I receive emails and messages on social media from people who state they are building a Blessing Box but are never heard from again. Years ago, a Girl Scout troop sent me photos of the Box they had built, but it never made it out into the community, and I never heard from them again.

Once this effort was launched, it continued to take on a life of its own. Things I had not considered initially not only seemed to make sense but also morphed into the norm. For example, I had thought that with a small network of Boxes, I would visit each site periodically and monitor the Box's status. I quickly realized that a working mother with active kids, a spouse, a home, and a dog to keep up with would not be able to keep up with more than a dozen Boxes as well. Luckily, all the hosts and folks who signed on to be part of our Project were committed, and my personal visits were unnecessary.

There were other challenges and growing pains we had to work through as well, some of which still crop up from time to time.

Competing Pantries

Another problem I did not anticipate was competing pantries, which I touched on earlier. Now that we have an established network of locations, we are frequently contacted by folks who want to set up a Blessing Box somewhere specific such as their church. After we ask them to look at our map so they do not put it near another existing location, some of these hosts decide to put it at their desired location regardless of our concern. At least twice, different groups have decided to set up Blessing Boxes directly across the street from each other.

I fear that these people are missing the point of anonymous giving. If a pantry already exists near where you were thinking of placing one, then you can use your efforts and funds to fill the existing Box. This movement is not about creating a show of giving or making something of your own to be able to post on your social media accounts. Anonymous giving is supposed to be the opposite of these types of performative activism. However, while I will do a lot of things to further this mission, I am not going to fight with church ladies. So instead, when this occurs I thank them but do not put the Boxes down as separate locations on our map. I don't want to confuse anyone who is looking for something to eat.

Keeping the Boxes Full

My involvement now is almost exclusively via my phone and computer, aside from trips to my local Boxes to donate and speaking engagements. I get lots of emails and messages on the Instagram and Facebook accounts with requests like, "Hey, could you make a post and tell people that the church over in Bonneau hasn't had any donations in a while?" When I get these messages and share that the Bonneau Blessing Box needs some attention, people who live in that community are reminded about the Box and become motivated to fill it up.

Most of the Boxes have been integrated into their communities such that I will see posts on hyperlocal social media accounts like, "Hey, has anybody been by the Blessing Box? I'm going to put some baby food in there today," or "I have formula and I'm going to put it in the Blessing Box." A lot of online communication by people who are local to a specific Box also makes a huge difference in keeping the Boxes full and maintained. I have also found that posting photos of empty Boxes goes a lot further toward motivating people to donate than a post with only words to identify barren locations.

Occasionally, the Boxes at people's houses will end up having so many donations that they don't all fit inside, so the hosts will have to bring things into their house until the stock goes down a bit and they can refill. What a good problem to have! Sometimes, the more engaged hosts can tell when they need to stagger the contents so they can ensure more than one person is getting access to the available food.

We nearly always see a dip in donations—or an uptick in their use, I'm not sure which since we cannot tell with anonymous giving—at the end of the month as people attempt to stretch their budgets until their next payday. Another predictable increase in activity at our Boxes comes around the time of natural disasters such as hurricanes, especially if evacuation or school closures become necessary. Learning these trends has helped me guide our messaging to solicit donations more aggressively during these circumstances.

Homeowners' Associations

One of our biggest obstacles has been homeowners' associations (HOA). So much so that it has been a standard answer for us to tell people who want to set up a Blessing Box in their neighborhoods with HOAs that before they even start building, they need to get clearance from their HOA. It is certainly easier to deal with them on the front end than argue with them once the Box is installed. One HOA officer called me several times after the initial installation of a Box in her neighborhood because she was furious and worried that the Box would impede traffic and become a dumping ground, but she relented after she realized how popular the idea was with the other residents.

Local government bureaucracy, zoning ordinances, and health departments have plagued some of the other pantry projects in other cities—but we haven't had that problem because we try to address all those concerns before adding a new pantry or extending into a new area of the state. We also have not placed any of our Boxes at chain retail stores or businesses that have corporate headquarters outside our local area.

Publicity

In the very beginning, we got a lot of great press. I did many interviews in a short period of time—print interviews, news interviews, and several internet-based talk show interviews. I think people can really get on board with the idea of anonymously giving food if they hear about the mission behind it, rather than if they learn about it for the first time by seeing a tiny structure with food in it. Being out there speaking about the mission assisted in our growth and smoothed over some of the questions that could have arisen about our purpose.

Social media presence has also helped because people get excited when they see our Boxes in real life if they are already familiar with the concept from seeing it online. Also, when they know the background, they already feel connected to the idea. I knew we really had made an impression when I was taking a break at work and saw that I had received a voicemail from the CEO of an international corporation while I was in court. He had read about our Project and wanted to thank me for helping to fight food insecurity. I saved the voicemail to play for my grandparents.

Food Safety and Quality

I would be remiss if I did not spend a little time discussing food safety, liability, and good practices when outlining some of our obstacles.[1] As a lawyer, it made me nervous that someone might try to take advantage of the generous and kind people who host these Boxes at their homes. I drafted a disclaimer to place on the Box, explaining that the items inside have been anonymously donated and that we do not warrant the contents of the items. This is especially important at the Free Fridges, where perishable foods can be donated and present a higher risk of food safety issues.

Our disclaimer states as follows:

DISCLAIMER: Items in this refrigerator/Blessing Box have been anonymously donated. Lowcountry Blessing Box Project (LCBB), property owners, renters, donors, volunteers, and others associated with LCBB are not responsible, assume no responsibility, and make no warranties for the contents or the quality of the items placed herein. Partake at your own risk. Responsibility is on the consumer to check expiration dates before use. LCBB and its associates and partners are not liable for any damages or losses associated with the use of this refrigerator/Blessing Box.

------

[1] This is not legal advice. Contact a local attorney to discuss any questions or concerns you may have about setting up or executing any type of anonymous giving endeavor.

I get complaints occasionally about the quality of the items in the Blessing Boxes, but thus far, we have resolved all those issues without much trouble. Usually, the person who contacts me has found something expired in the Box and wants me to be aware that they found it and threw it away. Expiration dates are the biggest and most frequent concern I hear about from our benefactors and some donors. We repeatedly state—on all our platforms—that we do not accept expired food. We also ask people not to donate food that has been opened or tampered with in any way. Not only are these foods a liability for us, but I also hate to think of the person who is already so down on their luck that they are getting food out of a Box to feed their family, and then once they summon the courage and humility to do that, the food they find is old, possibly spoiled, and not healthy to consume.

There is a federal law that was enacted to protect nonprofit organizations from liability when dealing with donated food and distributions to those in need. The Bill Emerson Good Samaritan Food Donation Act was intended to encourage the donation of food that may have otherwise gone to waste by limiting the criminal and civil liabilities of companies and other organizations that make food donations to nonprofit organizations.[2] Further, it protects citizens from liability when they have donated in good faith but their donations cause harm to the recipient.

Some of the host locations, especially those at houses of worship and small businesses, have added their pantries to their liability insurance. Other organizations have declined to become hosts because of concerns about potential liabilities. Many of our Blessing Boxes are at sites that do not have someone on the premises every day, like churches or businesses that are closed on the weekends. This works fine because nonperishable food is just

---

[2] Bill Emerson Good Samaritan Food Donation Act, 42 U.S.C. § 1791 (1996).

that—nonperishable, so if it sits in the Box for several days or even a week, it won't cause any harm to the quality of the items.

The Free Community Fridges are a different animal entirely. We take special precautions since these temperature-controlled Blessing Boxes receive donations of homemade soup, produce, dairy, and sometimes meat that cannot stay in the Fridge past its prime. We have gone so far as to pay someone in the community to look after one of the Free Fridges, and her duties include fully emptying, sanitizing, and reorganizing it at least once per week. I once received a message from someone who said the food in that Free Fridge had been there "for months," but due to our rigorous attention to that location, I am confident this person was mistaken. The cleaning routine gives us all peace of mind and ensures the safety of the shoppers at that location.

By not donating expired food and by instead giving our best, we make our neighbors and community members see that we value them. By leaving items that have been in our pantries for years, we may help someone eat, but we send a message that the recipients are not worthy of "new" food. This is a slippery slope because we do not want to shame anyone for their ability to give. We are grateful for all our supporters in any capacity, but because of the reasons I've stated here, we prefer to accept only up-to-date goods.

Box Placement

I receive many messages asking for help in duplicating my Project in other cities. I don't think there is a secret recipe for success, and some of what has worked for me in the South did not work for my sister's Blessing Box Project in the Midwest. One of the most frequent questions is about where to put them. Will it bring homeless people into our neighborhood? What if the neighbors are mad about it? The oversimplified answer is that you should put them where you think they will help people.

Here are some thoughts on Blessing Box placement if you are just getting started:

- Think about where people go to seek other types of assistance, like the public defender's office, libraries, senior centers, and housing assistance offices. Can you place your pantry at or near any of those types of locations?
- If you're in the South, try to place it in the shade.
- Unless the Box i in an urban area with heavy foot traffic, it needs to be where people in cars can access it safely and without impeding the flow of traffic. Make sure there is enough room to pull off the road to load and unload from the Box.
- Try to share your vision with your neighbors and get them on board with the mission before you install the pantry—things will be a lot smoother that way. Help clear up any misconceptions they may have about who the pantry is meant to help.
- One misconception is that the Boxes are used only by homeless people. But not all homeless people are similarly situated, and people who are hungry are not always homeless. They might drive a nice car but be in the midst of an ugly divorce. They might be wearing nice shoes but be paying huge medical debt. They might be elderly and on a fixed income or young and recently unemployed. In fact, there are arguably more resources and avenues for assistance for people who are homeless than for those who are employed but either do not make more than minimum wage or have fallen into hard times for a variety of reasons.

Emptying the Box

Since I started the Blessing Box Project, one of the most unexpected things I have discovered is that people who have the least to give often are giving the most, and the people with the least resources are usually the ones who are taking exactly what they need to get by and not a bit more. We also have found that those living on the margins, often living transiently or in groups in wooded areas or under overpasses, will come to the Blessing Boxes to collect food not just for themselves, but for their group. We often ask our supporters to recognize the possibility that just because one person empties an entire Box does not mean they are being selfish. The likelihood is high that they are taking the items to feed not just themselves or their families, but an entire group of similarly situated people.

We had a situation where someone followed a family who had "completely emptied" the Box, took photos of them and their car—which included the license plate—and posted the photos on social media. This attempt to shame people for taking something free is the opposite of our Project's mission. Apparently, the person who posted the pictures had spoken to the family, who said they intended to mail the food to family members in another country. Even if this were true—which is doubtful because it would cost far more to ship those food items than to buy them—it should not matter. I suspect instead that the person saw a family who didn't "look American" and decided to shame them in this way.

I am careful to remind those who are part of our Project that anonymous giving is not for everyone—and that is completely okay. Many organizations feed people and collect data on who those people are and what their income situation is, then use a system to "assess their need." We are not one of them. If you're more comfortable knowing that your donations went to someone who "really needed them," then maybe our Project is not your cup of tea. I hope you will not be discouraged and will donate to another organization. However, we operate on a no-judgment, no-shame, no-questions approach. This approach cannot change, or the heart of the Project is lost.

Some locations in our network have posted signs that limit the number of items people are supposed to take at a time. Other locations have signs on the Boxes that tell people their actions are being monitored by cameras. Neither of these approaches fits with what I had in mind when I started this Project. However, one of the costs of explosive growth has been that I have had to let go of controlling this type of messaging. I didn't build the Boxes with these signs, nor did I ask their hosts to put them up. Many of them I have not even seen in person. So, I don't think it's in my purview to try to regulate their messaging, particularly when the Boxes are at churches or businesses.

I have been told that one church has not only a sign on its Box telling people to take only two or three items, but also that a small contingent of people sit at the Box to watch who takes things. The shoppers at this Box are terrified to use it. They feel bad enough getting food for their kids out of a random wooden box, but having to face an inquisition while they do it is too much. I hope that those engaging in this type of action reconsider and stop. Again, anonymous giving is not for everyone—and that is okay.

Chapter 7: What Is Food Insecurity?

Once upon a time, there was an old man who used to go to the ocean to do his writing. He had a habit of walking on the beach every morning before he began his work. Early one morning, he was walking along the shore after a big storm had passed and found the vast beach littered with starfish as far as the eye could see, stretching in both directions.

Off in the distance, the old man noticed a small boy approaching. As the boy walked, he paused every so often, and as he grew closer, the man could see that he was occasionally bending down to pick up an object and throw it into the sea. The boy came closer and the man called out, "Good morning! May I ask what it is that you are doing?"

The young boy paused, looked up, and replied, "Throwing starfish into the ocean. The tide has washed them up onto the beach and they can't return to the sea by themselves," the youth replied. "When the sun gets high, they will die, unless I throw them back into the water."

The old man replied, "But there must be tens of thousands of starfish on this beach. I'm afraid you won't really be able to make much of a difference."

The boy bent down, picked up yet another starfish, and threw it as far as he could into the ocean. Then he turned, smiled, and said, "It made a difference to that one!"

—"The Star Thrower," Anonymous

Food insecurity is a lack of consistent access to enough food for an active, healthy life. The United States Department of Agriculture

(USDA) defines very low food security as a situation wherein "food intake of household members is reduced and their normal eating patterns are disrupted because the household lacks money and other resources for food" at certain times during the year.[1]

Food insecurity is not the same as hunger. Hunger is a personal, physical sensation within an individual's body, but food insecurity encompasses a lack of financial resources to obtain food at the household level. Food insecurity is not knowing that you will be able to stretch your available resources out long enough to feed your family before your source of income is replenished. Simply put, food insecurity is not knowing that you will have enough money or resources to feed your family between now and your next paycheck.

I frequently share a graphic of a banana that I think clarifies the definition of food insecurity. The banana is cut into five pieces and labeled with the days of the week. The Monday piece is the largest, with each day after becoming increasingly smaller. The Friday piece is so small that it is barely visible.

Studies show adults with food insecurity will skip meals or reduce their portions to provide for children in their homes as they wait for payday. Many food insecure families do not qualify for assistance from food banks or are hesitant to turn to food banks due to the stigma. One "bad month" can be enough to plunge a household into food insecurity. Layoffs, unexpected car maintenance, unforeseen medical bills, or an accident on the job can suddenly force a family to choose between buying food and paying bills. This is the purpose of our Project—to bridge this gap while empowering the community to provide for our neighbors.

---

[1] Economic Research Service, U.S. Department of Agriculture, accessed February 21, 2021, https://www.ers.usda.gov/topics/food-nutrition-assistance/food-security-in-the-us/definitions-of-food-security.aspx.

Food insecurity is not the same as poverty. Some people living below the poverty line do not have food insecurity because they access various programs and services to ensure there will be food in their home. Conversely, some people who make more money than the poverty guidelines are food insecure because their resources do not cover their monthly bills. The issue is complex and relates to other factors such as affordable housing, the cost of medical care, and, in some cases, the cost of childcare.

One misconception regarding the purpose of our Boxes is that they are meant to be used only by homeless people. However, they are meant for whoever needs food. Many people who are hungry are not homeless. More resources and avenues for assistance exist for people who are homeless than for those who are employed but either do not make more than minimum wage or have fallen into hard times for a variety of reasons.

The Blessing Box Project operates on the belief that people are inherently kind and want to help others, but sometimes it is difficult to find tangible ways to put that desire into action. This is a local, direct way of helping people in our community. Whether it is a bag of rice, a picture colored by a child, or a pack of diapers, the recipient's day will be brighter because of the generosity of a stranger.

Because our Project is entirely anonymous, we do not know how many people benefit from our Blessing Boxes, how many people donate, and how often or how much food cycles through them each month. By simple math, if we assume that each of the two hundred Boxes in our network allows five people to eat per week, then we are feeding one thousand people per week and 52,000 people per year. This is a conservative estimate—some of our Boxes are so busy that they probably have five people taking food out every day. What we do know for certain, however, is that food insecurity is a real problem that we can directly address in small increments with a little kindness and a lot of community cooperation.

Hunger Is a Complex Problem

Food insecurity is a tiny part of the massive problem of hunger in modern society. Blessing Boxes are not intended and do not purport to solve hunger issues, lack of access to fresh, healthy foods for marginalized communities, or any other large-scale food-related issues facing us as a nation. The resources on these topics are plentiful and often political with deep dives into their roots in racism, classism, gentrification, and other systemic problems. This is not our lane, but it is our problem. And it should be everyone's concern.

Solutions to these large-scale problems must be investigated and supported by every single one of us. Food should not be a privilege. Kids should not be hungry at school. Adults should not have to choose between paying the rent and buying groceries. We should be talking about food deserts, but also about food apartheid. To be a part of the larger conversation, we must understand these terms and continue to research how to be part of the solution.

A food desert is defined by the Healthy Food Financing Initiative Working Group as "a low-income census tract where a substantial number or share of residents has low access to a supermarket or large grocery store."[2] Essentially, it is an area where people live without nearby access to a store that carries healthy foods. Have you ever noticed that there are plenty of convenience stores in

---

[2] Economic Research Service, U.S. Department of Agriculture, accessed February 22, 2021, https://www.ers.usda.gov/webdocs/DataFiles/80591/archived_documentation.pdf?v=0.

lower-income neighborhoods, but no stores that carry organic produce?

The term *food apartheid* takes a further step back to look at the food system while also accounting for issues of racial and income inequalities.[3] Unhealthy and processed foods are often the go-to meals for people in underserved neighborhoods because that is what is available within walking distance to their homes. That type of diet often leads to food-related illnesses such as diabetes, hypertension, and heart disease. "These illnesses then fuel the healthcare system's remedy, which is often medications and surgery over prevention. It's a vicious cycle."[4]

In addition to encouraging anonymous giving, we must also support the efforts of local urban farmers, food justice activists, and leaders who recognize that a sustainable solution needs to be found without any further delay. Research the ongoing work of your local urban farms and support the heroes who are doing the heavy lifting on these pervasive issues. We have several wonderful organizations in our area, and it has been a priority of mine to amplify their missions, their fundraisers, and their messages.

Donating to an anonymous pantry might make your heart feel good, but we are kidding ourselves if we think it is solving anything in the long term. Little Free Pantries and Blessing Boxes are merely a bandage on a deep wound.

The COVID-19 pandemic is creating permanent changes to the food systems of the world—everything from where your food comes

---

[3] "Food Apartheid | Why We Should Change the Way We Talk about Food Deserts," Jenae Ridge, The Green Urban Lunch Box, published June 16, 2020, accessed February 22, 2021, https://thegreenurbanlunchbox.com/food-apartheid-why-we-should-change-the-way-we-talk-about-food-deserts/.
[4] Ridge, "Food Apartheid."

from to how it's handled and the prices we pay. Everyone is encountering some level of food insecurity—some people for the first time. During the shutdown periods of 2020, grocery stores workers were—rightfully so—considered frontline workers. People were fistfighting over toilet paper. Many people had money to buy groceries but were too afraid to go into the store. We were panicked over our food supply, even if we were lucky enough to keep our income stream uninterrupted.

My sincere hope is that people took a brief pause to sit with that feeling of not knowing where the next meal for your family would come from. That is a feeling that millions of our fellow citizens experienced every single day, even in a prepandemic world. This is and was a chance to acquire some empathy, to think about the lived experience of others, and to build an understanding of food insecurity.

Giving Your Best

As I mentioned earlier, I have always encouraged people to give their best to the Boxes, not only their leftovers. I repeatedly remind our supporters not to donate open or expired food. This is a surprisingly controversial request. Many, many commenters on the Project's social media argue this point when I post a reminder, saying that food may still be safe to eat past the label's expiration date. I have read articles about scientific research that say the same, and it may be—in limited circumstances—true. However, I see this as a two-pronged issue: (1) it is a liability to donate open and/or expired food, and (2) it is not helpful to a person in need to receive something they cannot use.

So, I continue to remind folks that the Blessing Boxes are not the place to take food that you have cleaned out of your deceased relative's pantry that expired five years ago, nor are they the place to bring something you already opened but decided not to use. It is not helpful to give someone who needs assistance something that will disappoint them because they are unable to use it. This should not be construed as thinking that the shoppers at the Boxes are ungrateful. They are human. They might have food allergies, or kids who eat like . . . kids. Their inability to afford the items they would purchase for themselves and their families in this moment should not be a judgment on them, and arguing that they should be grateful for whatever they find in the Box on a given day contradicts the spirit of our Project.

I read an article written by someone who had experienced food insecurity as a child, and she addressed this issue of giving your best. "The biggest problem with poverty is the shame that comes with it. When you give the best you have to someone in need, it translates into something much deeper to the receiver. It means they are worthy. If it's not good enough for you, it's not good enough for those in need either. Giving the best you have does more than feed an empty belly—it feeds the soul."[5]

Anticipating Needs

Because giving the same canned goods can get repetitive, and to build a feeling of community during the holiday season, I encourage people to make up Thanksgiving Bags that have everything needed for a traditional Thanksgiving feast except the turkey: gravy mix, mashed potatoes, pie crusts, canned green beans, corn, and more. This can also turn out as a great way to get kids involved by drawing pictures on the outsides of the paper grocery bags. I also help

---

[5] Kristine Levine, "I'm a Little Too Fat, a Little Too Giving. I Think I Know Why: Using the Hunger I Experienced as a Kid to Teach Mine the Power of Generosity," Medium, January 17, 2019, https://humanparts.medium.com/i-am-a-little-too-fat-im-a-little-too-generous-i-think-i-know-why-e97cd25b7eeb.

people organize "reverse Advent calendars" by collecting an item a day for the weeks leading up to Christmas. During Lent, I promote the collection of forty days' worth of items to be donated on Easter.

I try to encourage everyone involved in our Project to anticipate the needs in the community and respond to those needs directly—for example, donating sunscreen in December is appreciated but also not the best use of resources at that exact time. To focus in on the community's needs, I have tried to gather anonymous feedback. A couple of times, I put a dry erase board in the pantry closest to my house, but each time, someone took it before we (at least, before I) got any messages or requests on it. I have seen this notebook/whiteboard approach be more successful at some of our other locations. At least one of the Boxes in our network has almost a sign-in, sign-out kind of thing going on, which I haven't encouraged elsewhere because it seems to remove the anonymity. However, I can see why that host finds it useful. Part of the growing pains of an ever-expanding project is that just because I do not like an approach does not mean it is incorrect—and it's not mine to control.

Perhaps the best way to communicate these specific needs is via social media or email. I have had mothers email me to ask for a loaf of bread and a jar of peanut butter to get them through until payday. I also frequently get messages and emails asking for a specific Blessing Box to be refilled. I try to post on social media when I hear about one that has been chronically empty. While I am confident that those posts do spur people into action and get the Box filled up, I am honestly not sure if word of it being filled ever reaches the actual person who emailed to request it. Again, this is one of the trade-offs of the anonymous giving model.

But Do They Really "Need" It?

One of the most common questions I have received since the beginning of this Project is what can be done about a shopper who is either perceived to be or actually taking everything out of a Box all in one trip. This concern has been voiced by hosts, by donors, and also by commenters on social media posts about the Project. My standard response is that that person must have needed everything. Your definition of "need" might not be the same as mine, but we are not participating in this Project to determine who is worthy of food and who is not. Nor are we coming back for the items we place inside the Box as donations. The spirit of the giving must match the anonymity of the Project, and food insecurity is complicated. Those in need do not always look downtrodden.

After the "must-have-needed-it" response comes my secondary standard answer, which is, "Have you talked to the person emptying the Box?" Often people don't realize what the Boxes are or that other community members are stocking them out of their own generosity. Sometimes people are in an unexpected but dire situation, and their needs far outweigh the level of assistance a free food pantry with inconsistent and random food items is equipped to provide. Those people need information on where to turn for a more permanent and predictable way to obtain food for themselves and their families.

Several times a conversation with the person who was taking many items at a time led him to get connected to a church with a food pantry that is open several times a week as well as a community organization that offers assistance with rental payments. If we make assumptions and do not ask any questions, we are passing up chances to make more of an impact.

The third response to this "taking-everything" problem is for the host and donors to not stock the Box fully. Sometimes shoppers are using the Boxes as if they were grocery stores, and it is impossible to tell the difference between someone who just does not want to go to the store and someone who cannot afford to go to the store. By the very nature of the Project, we cannot discern the needy from the greedy, nor should we try. The hosts of the Boxes know their normal rhythms. Some Boxes are filled and emptied multiple times a day; others might take a week for their contents to be gone, and still others sit close to empty most of the time.

If a host starts seeing a Box that is full and then completely empty within a few hours when that is not normally the case, we suggest stocking it only half full for a while or stocking it every few days. This seems to help prevent shoppers from taking everything at once. We also discourage putting grocery bags in the Boxes for people to take things out; when bags are available, people take more at a time.

Finally, some hosts believe people are taking items from the Boxes only to return them for cash at local stores. I hesitate to include this because I do not want to introduce the possibility that this is happening for hosts who might not have considered it before. Although I don't have any personal knowledge as to whether or not this happens, I do think it is rare if it does. However, the hosts who think this is happening at their locations have sometimes decided to mark through the bar codes on the packages with a permanent marker to notify store clerks that the items have been donated. I don't know whether this stops Box shoppers from taking food to return it, but it is a potential approach to consider.

More Than Just Food

A common misconception of our Project is that the food is solely intended for unhoused people. It is meant for whoever might need something on that particular day. However, I have learned that some items are particularly appreciated by folks who do not have regular access to a kitchen. These items include bottled water, cans with pop-tops rather than cans that require a can opener, nutritious foods rather than snack foods, ready-to-eat meals, socks, protein sources such as canned chicken or tuna, and manual can openers.

Several years ago, I received a message from an unhoused man, and over time he and I have kept in touch. When I get bulk donations of socks, I reach out to him to help me distribute them. I am pleased to report that he now has a house, but he has taught me valuable lessons on how to help those who do not. He gave me a deeper understanding of what resources are available to unhoused people and where the biggest struggles lie. For example, he has been employed the entire time I have known him, and he usually gets to work on his bicycle.

Recently, however, someone ran over his bicycle, and he has been unable to replace it. When he did not have a house, he relied on his bike to get to his secret place where he laid his head each night and to a nearby strip mall to charge his phone on an exterior wall outlet. He also used his bicycle to get to work and to get food out of a local Blessing Box. Without that transportation option, everything else in his life was on hold, so it was one of his highest priorities to secure a new bicycle. His insights, and his willingness to share them with me, have helped me understand how to better serve similarly situated people.

The success of my Project highlights our nation's failures to effectively address food insecurity as an issue plaguing so many. The fact that there are so many people covertly taking food out of tiny structures because they cannot afford to provide for their families is not something we should celebrate. While I very much appreciate all the donors and supporters of my Project, I hope that we do not take our collective eye off the ball. We must continue to insist that the systemic problems with food access are addressed.

Chapter 8: Free Community Fridges

Until mid-2019, we could only accept donations of nonperishable foods. It's hot in the Lowcountry and food spoils quickly—even in the winter. When I saw a news article about a church in Pittsburgh that installed a refrigerated free pantry, my newest goal was set.

By searching online secondhand appliance sites, I found a restaurant going out of business and made a lowball offer on an industrial refrigerator with sliding glass doors and plenty of shelves. They weren't able to accept my offer, but luckily our donors were able to supplement what we had in the bank so we could purchase our first Free Community Fridge. Now we could take donations of milk, eggs, homemade soup, meats, produce, and so many other perishable goods and allow them to be anonymously redistributed with no questions asked.

The Free Community Fridge concept has widely expanded our reach for donors. For example, a local nonprofit that makes soup and gives it away now donates some for our refrigerator. A couple of farms have been donating produce. Some of our hosts and volunteers who have connections with bakeries get bread products to put them. I am thrilled to be able to offer a healthier and wider variety of options for our shoppers than just nonperishables. As I've mentioned, underserved communities are often food deserts without access to fresh fruits and vegetables, and the Fridges allow us to anonymously donate produce.

The placement of the Free Community Fridges has been key to their success—the first one is at a neighborhood resource center that gets daily visits from the founders and volunteers. We placed it on the center's covered porch so that it can be plugged in and will not get wet when it rains. Our organization also helps them pay for a weekly cleaning, sanitizing, and reorganization of the contents. The second one is at our area's only pay-as-you-can café, and the third Fridge is located at a thrift store.

Throughout the COVID-19 pandemic, I began seeing many more refrigerated Blessing Boxes pop up around the country, especially in larger urban areas. Some have even partnered with local artists, so not only are they giving away temperature-controlled foods anonymously, but they are also creating public art spaces. Swoon. Talk about #goals!

Hopefully, the future of our Project will bring more Free Community Fridges to our network. There are different hurdles with the Fridges than with the traditional Blessing Boxes; for example, the placement is more complicated because they must be plugged in, need protection from the elements, and are much more likely to be stolen. The potential liabilities are greater too. Despite the extra challenges, I think that Free Community Fridges are the future of the anonymous giving movement.

Since creating this project, I have learned a great deal about the concept of mutual aid and I think the refrigerators, more so than the Blessing Boxes, reflect this concept. Mutual aid is a form of solidarity-based support, in which communities unite against a common struggle, rather than leaving individuals to fend for themselves[1]. Mutual aid calls on people to work cooperatively to meet everyone's needs. It differs from charity in that charity is a one-way relationship between an organization and recipients, and frequently responds to the effects of inequality but not its causes. Mutual aid is an act of solidarity that builds sustained networks between neighbors.[2]

Mutual aid efforts have long existed in underserved community and are often run by women of color. If I had the understanding of mutual aid when I began this project four years ago that I now possess, I do not believe I would have ever incorporated it as a non-profit. My hope is that someday, with some large changes, what I have built can become more authentically a mutual-aid effort rather than a charity. The spirit of my project fits better into a system of solidarity than into the hierarchy of a non-profit organization.

---

[1] "So You Want to Get Involved in Mutual Aid," Amanda Arnold, The Cut, published September 30, 2020, accessed May 4, 2021, https://www.thecut.com/2020/09/what-exactly-is-mutual-aid-how-to-get-involved.html

[2] Arnold, "So You Want to Get Involved in Mutual Aid."

Raising Awareness through Mutual Aid

Many people believe that anonymously giving food is not an act of charity but one based in mutual aid. During the pandemic, the number of food insecure people has soared and brought into focus the very real problem of hunger for underemployed people, students, the elderly, and so many more. The pandemic has also shown us that most of us are just an unfortunate step or two away from food insecurity—a lost job, a medical crisis, or a divorce could put many of us shopping at the Boxes we were donating to just a short time ago.

One misconception about food insecurity is that there is not enough food for everyone. But if you read research on food waste, you'll come to see that the problem is often not a lack of food—it's that the food we have is not being directed to the people who need it. Community fridges allow their hosts to partner with local restaurants, supermarkets, urban farmers, and food pantries to have a place where they can donate excess goods.

Free Community Fridges, like Blessing Boxes, are not a solution to the problem of food insecurity or to the problem of food waste. They are a small-scale way to address these issues and temporarily assist with the larger problem. However, and perhaps just as importantly, they are bringing attention to the citizens who are volunteering their time and efforts to this cause, which in turn is shining a light on the systemic problems that underlie food insecurity in our communities. Hopefully, enough attention will attract the eyes and ears of those with the power to change our nation's policies on food waste, food insecurity, food deserts, and access to fresh, healthy food for all communities.

Free Community Fridges, Little Free Pantries, and Blessing Boxes are physical reminders in our neighborhoods that the community cares about one another. That we are looking out for each other's well-being so much so that we are willing to feed you, no questions asked and for as long as you need, because you are part of the community and you have value. Sending this message not only helps those who are taking the food, but it also shows our leaders that the community has done its part—the leaders must also step up and do theirs.

Chapter 9: The Power of Anonymous Giving

"But when you give to the needy, do not let your left hand know what your right hand is doing, so that your giving may be in secret. Then your Father, who sees what is done in secret, will reward you."— Matthew 6:3–4, NIV

The concepts of anonymous giving and/or mutual aid are not for everyone—and that is okay. As I mentioned it earlier in the book—this type of giving will not appeal to all. Some of us prefer to imagine who is being helped by our generosity rather than knowing the specifics. Or maybe you feel like it would be easier not to judge the people your donations will go to if you know the general situation they are facing, like when you donate to charities who help teenage mothers or homeless veterans.

There is power in generosity and even more power when you choose to give your gifts without expecting acknowledgment, praise, or thanks. The most altruistic thing I can think of is giving without the prospect of receiving anything in return.

The quantity of an anonymous gift does not matter. Maybe you put hundreds of dollars' worth of food in a Blessing Box each week or decide that you'll anonymously drop a five-dollar bill in a public bathroom to delight the next person who comes along. The most meaningful monetary donation that this Project has ever received came from the most unexpected place—a Lowcountry native who was serving a fifteen-year prison sentence. I will never forget receiving a check in the mail from the department of corrections. Giving generously regardless of your net worth is healthy for our minds and our spirits. It is like our little secret with the universe.

In my professional life when I am feeling down or dissatisfied with a certain case or project I've been working on, I have found the best way to get myself back on track is to volunteer my time. I've done this through judging mock-trial competitions, taking on a mentee from the Bar Association, and speaking at seminars for law students. Recentering my gratitude always helps me get back to an appreciation for my work.

Likewise, sneaky kindness always makes me happy—like around the holidays when some anonymous donor pays for all the toys that parents have put on layaway or someone paying off a heap of past-due library fees. I love this quote from Bob Kerrey: "Unexpected kindness is the most powerful, least costly, and most underrated agent of human change." What better way to inspire others to help their neighbors than by making it really easy—and what could be easier than dropping extra food into a Box on the side of the road when it is convenient for you to do so, without having to tell a single other soul about it? (The answer, I discovered several months into this Project, is an Amazon wish list that ships items directly to one of the most used locations. The only thing easier than visiting a BB on your own schedule is donating from your couch in your pajamas using your phone.)

Maybe you want to give but are wondering, 'What if someone comes and steals everything?' Anonymous giving is not about us wasting time wondering or policing or judging. If that is where your mind goes, then anonymous giving might not be for you—and again, that's okay. There are plenty of other organizations that do amazing work and would be grateful for your support.

The idea of anonymous giving can be simply boiled down to this: we are doing things for people not because of who they are, but because of who we are. It doesn't matter who the recipient is. If they are getting something out of the Box, they need it. Maybe they don't need it today. Maybe they don't "need" it by someone else's standards, but something—somewhere in their head—is telling them that they need this item right now, and the why is not for us to know or judge.

Our local food bank has a program where organizations can sign up to receive their donated food, but since we don't have any data and are completely anonymous, we do not qualify as a distribution point. I don't know how many people are using the pantries. I don't know if it's the same person five times a week shopping a Box or if it's five different people during the week. We cannot meet the food bank's application standards because I can't tell them whom we're feeding, nor do I want to. That is what makes us different, and I don't want to break that wall where we know anything about who's coming to get food. It is very important to me that everything stays anonymous.

Making Anonymous Giving Easy

Because it is easy to anonymously participate in the Blessing Box Project, people do. You can buy nonperishable foods when you're doing your own shopping, and you can leave them in your car for however long it takes until it is convenient to drop them at your local Box—they will not go bad. Because you do not have to sign up for a time or day to donate, you do not have to tell anyone what you donated or how much. There is an ease in participating that is lacking in so many other areas of our lives.

Take parent participation for school events. Even though it's generally fairly simple, sending the items I signed up for on the correct day does not always happen, despite my best intentions. God bless the Pinterest parents of the world. I am not among your number, and I am grateful for you, because someone has to send the Halloween-themed cupcakes decorated to perfection while I'm over here barely remembering to toss the paper napkins in my kid's bookbag as she runs out the door in the morning.

The simplicity and the ease of this Project are what makes it successful. I truly believe that people are inherently good and want to help others. Even so, we often think we are too busy to do anything. Intentionally or not, we wear our busyness like a badge of honor:

"How have you been?"

"Oh, I'm doing great, just—you know—really busy."

"We should hang out!"

"Yes, I'd love to, but life has just been so crazy lately."

"Work is just so busy."

How many times have we had similar conversations? The beauty of the Blessing Box Project from a donor's point of view is that the Boxes are there at the ready for whenever you're ready, available, and willing to participate. And your participation can be as simple or as complicated as you make it. You can drive around for two weeks with cans bumping around in the back of your car until you have a few minutes to stop by a Box, or you can organize a large-scale food drive with your entire neighborhood and advertise it in all your networks.

Many times over, I had no idea that people had taken the latter approach. My husband came home from work one day and told me that he saw an electronic billboard on the highway seeking donations to a neighborhood HOA food drive for the Blessing Boxes. For me, as the founder and as a formerly "very busy" person, I consider this my biggest success. The Kindness Army has taken hold. They are doing their own things—large and small, loudly and quietly, sometimes for acknowledgment but often without anyone knowing.

Chapter 10: How to Build a Kindness Army

As the popularity of my Project grew, I felt the need to harness the power of all people who were paying attention to what I created into something more than food donations. I thought about whose work in the community was not being fully appreciated and honored. I contemplated what organization's efforts I wanted to amplify with the reach of the Blessing Box social media pages. Fresh Future Farm, my favorite urban farm, kept popping into my thoughts because I have always been in awe of their founder. She took a vacant city block and turned it into a productive farm and community hub.[1]

First, I encouraged people to volunteer with and donate to the farm, which is located in a community that has been a food desert for many years. I had volunteered there myself with friends and on some occasions had taken my children along with me. It is an incredible feat of ingenuity and I wanted everyone who knew about the Blessing Boxes to know about the work being done at Fresh Future Farm. I consider the farm and its creators to be the gold standard in the front-line fight for food justice.

The Blessing Box Project was able to sponsor several kids to attend Farm Camp in the summer. I made it a point to consistently boost all the farm's events and social media posts because while the Blessing Box Project can operate with very little overhead cost, a farm needs donors and volunteers.

Through one of our Blessing Box hosts, I became connected to a neighborhood resource center in an underserved area. I used the

---

[1] Learn more about Fresh Future Farm at www.freshfuturefarm.org.

Blessing Box Project's reach to organize a book drive to benefit their students. Our effort resulted in more than one hundred donated books. Next, as an organization, we participated in several school supply drives throughout the tri-county area and encouraged folks to donate supplies through our Blessing Boxes as well. The more events like this that we participated in, the more community partners we acquired, and the more our reach grew.

Aside from expanding our community impact with other organizations, people were getting involved in the Blessing Box Project in unique ways beyond my original vision. A musician reached out to tell me that he was going to raise money for the Project by running and livestreaming it while he asked people to give money for the whole time he was running. He ran thirty miles and gave us $800! That money translated into many online grocery orders during the COVID-19 quarantine.

A mother who lost a child donates each month on the day he passed in his honor. One group of our volunteers exercises by doing a "Box-to-Box Ruck" where they fill backpacks with canned goods and then walk or run these bags to our various Blessing Boxes. Our volunteers have hosted canned food drives at grocery stores, and schools and churches have held food drives to benefit us as well. We have volunteers who organize "yard gives" that require shoppers to bring food donations in exchange for items from the event rather than paying for them.

There are so many other examples I could cite about people really making this Project into their own personal crusade, and each of them inspires me anew when I reflect back on all their innovative ideas.

About nine months into the Project, a tragedy struck one of our hosts. She was in the hospital, and her daughter was at her house preparing for her discharge when she got the call to go pick up her mom. In her daughter's haste to return to the hospital, she left the stove on and a fire started in their home. The host and I had not known each other long; we met when I dropped off the Blessing Box at her house and had stayed in touch since. Even though we weren't well acquainted, she reached out shortly after the fire to tell me what had happened. To this day I regret not driving to her house, offering to collect her entire family and bring them to my house to stay until things could be sorted out at their home. The day after she called, I started organizing a relief effort to help the host and her family replace their belongings and make the necessary repairs to their home.

Within a few days, the outreach effort taking place through our Blessing Box channels had netted lots of kitchen items, bedding, a sofa, and kitchen cabinets. I don't think I consciously thought about it at the time, but our Kindness Army was coming together. Along with a network of pantries, I had also created a network of people.

In this particular instance, someone was handling the cabinet installation, someone else was handling the legal aspects for the family, several people the host and I had never met were donating money, and others were providing the truck to pick up the couch someone gave but couldn't transport, all while someone else was cleaning and reorganizing the house. I was also able to get them new pillows and framed some family pictures to make it feel more like home.

This—the organization of like-minded people working toward a common goal—is the real power of the Lowcountry Blessing Box Project.

Prior to the coronavirus pandemic, we were having monthly lunches as a group at our area's only pay-what-you-can café.[2] This was a great way for the hosts, volunteers, donors, participants, and me to all come together regularly to discuss the Project but also to

---

[2] Learn more about Destiny Community Café at www.facebook.com/Destinycommunitycafe.

just generally enjoy one another's company. We are, after all, people with the same type of hearts. I thought this was also a great way to support the café, because they are on an amazing mission that aligns so well with our own. Destiny Community Cafe feeds everyone who comes in its doors, regardless of ability to pay. Patrons pay what they can for their meal, and if they're able, they may pay a little bit extra for the next person who comes in that needs a little help.

Because of our social media reach and the ever-growing number of people following our efforts, the Kindness Army continued to expand. The more connections we made and lives we touched, the more opportunities that presented themselves to spread kindness and build empathy in our community.

Building Community through Social Media

By far the most effective and least costly tool for spreading our message of anonymous giving and community building has been social media. My background is not in marketing, but I have learned an awful lot since I thought up the Blessing Box Project about how to reach people and what kind of messaging resonates. Generally, I've found a few things to be true: there are many crazy people on the internet, there are lots of really good people in the world, and there is an opportunity in social media to reach folks you never would have thought to target.

I use two main platforms—Instagram and Facebook. We also have a Twitter account that I have linked to the other two so my posts on Facebook or Instagram are automatically tweeted. I haven't made any conscious effort to grow a Twitter following, probably because I don't use it personally and therefore lack a certain comfort level and savvy with its functions.

For purposes of this Project, I have primarily focused on using Facebook for a few reasons. First of all, it is much easier to remain anonymous on Facebook than on Instagram. The only time you'll see my face on a Facebook post is when I am making a video at a live event—and that's because someone has to narrate what's going on. Generally, I pop on to the video to thank donors and provide event information; for example: "Thank you for donating; we are at Community Baptist Church on Main Street giving out turkeys from 10:00 a.m. to 5:00 p.m." I follow many other pantry projects on social media and have noticed that the organizers either take the approach I'm describing here—where their faces and names are largely absent—or swing entirely in the other direction, not only showing their faces but also thanking individual donors by name.

Second, the audience on Facebook is older than the users on Instagram. I joined Facebook when you had to have a .edu email address to get an account. These days our elementary school teachers are on Facebook along with our grandparents. The average age of the people interacting with our content across all platforms is over 35, so Facebook is where more of our target audience is spending their online time.

I do not think there is a correct way or an incorrect way to engage with social media followers. It has been important to me that the Blessing Box Project stay as anonymous as possible, but this is strictly a personal choice based on my own philosophy. I chose this approach in part because I was concerned that someone would think the Project was created just to be a platform for me to seek attention or praise. That could not be further from the truth, and that is also, largely, the purpose of this book. If I can put all the information I've learned over the years out into the public domain, then I can fade into the background.

I see a lot of engagement with the posts giving a sort of daily update by pantry hosts in other cities around the country—they stand by their pantry and say what is in stock that day, what they are low on, or even who came by to donate things that week. As I said, this is not the approach I have embraced, but I think it has been successful too. As a practical matter, I could never keep up with the daily status of all our locations even if I tried.

I do not make a lot of "pantry status" posts, but I do make an exception for pictures of kids donating to the Blessing Boxes when parents or grandparents send them to me. I like to post them—with permission, of course!—because they get a lot of engagement and interaction. Also, it is important that parents encourage their kids to get involved in giving back and to help grow their empathy, and donating to our Boxes is a very easy and effective way to do just that.

Instagram is a different animal entirely. Admittedly, I did not focus on Instagram until well after I had already found success on Facebook, and I am certainly still learning. Our Instagram following is about 10 percent of our Facebook following. On Facebook, you can share your post in groups and find new followers in the group. I have not figured out a similar way to share posts as widely on Instagram.

Since the Project began, with each new Blessing Box I do a series of updates. Each new Box gets an ANNOUNCEMENT post, then I add the location to Google Maps and to our location list, which is always pinned to the top of our Facebook page. I add the photo provided by the new host to our Facebook photo album of all the Boxes, and I share a post reiterating that it is an anonymous food donation site where anyone can leave what they can or take what they need. Repeating the purpose of the Box in the announcement post ensures that if someone sees it for the first time on a friend's timeline, they will know what it is for—and not confuse it for a Little Free Library.

Along with this routine for new Boxes, I also share the announcement post in Facebook group pages specific to the area of town or neighborhood where the host had placed the Box. This gives the neighbors the opportunity to know what it is and why it's there, and most importantly, they are encouraged to feel some ownership over it. Because they are among the first to know, they might also tell their other neighbors and friends. They (hopefully) also feel engaged enough to clean out trash, kill any bugs they see, and take their kids to the store to replenish it when it gets low.

This specificity of sharing is made easy through Facebook groups, but the only comparable approach on Instagram that I am aware of is through hashtagging or tagging the location, which I do not think has the same level of reach.

I've found that the best way to gain traction on Instagram is through the Stories feature, which disappear from public view after twenty-four hours. The more often you post Stories, the more frequently your account will pop to the front of your followers' feeds, so near-constant engagement by the poster is necessary to be successful. However, because there is not that much content to post to the Stories without adding some personal touches, I feel like I reveal myself much more on Instagram than on Facebook and lose some anonymity.

Still, Stories are a fun way to engage with followers—you can post polls and ask questions, among other things. I also use them to share other organizations' upcoming events without clogging up our account with activities that are important to share but not necessarily related to our Project directly.

I am definitely not a social media influencer, but I do have some tips on making videos and other high-quality content to engage your audience:

- Make high-quality videos so that your viewers want to watch videos in their entirety. Make sure your photos are high quality too. Don't wiggle the camera or take a video in a dark room. Don't take photos of your Boxes at night, or if you do, use a flash.
- If you're doing a video, stay on message—do not talk to people off camera, ramble about something unrelated, or apologize for

your appearance or how messy your house looks. That is not why the person tuned in to listen to you.

- If you're filming a video to post on social media, think about what you're going to say before you begin filming. If you need to, make some notes or bullet points to refer to while you are filming. My courtroom experience has served me very well when it comes to making social media videos because I have been standing up and talking to a judge or a jury for so long, I am very comfortable speaking in public. This will not be true for everyone, and if you are not accustomed to it, it can be daunting. Plan your message and stick to it.

- Keep in mind that the person viewing your video or reading your post might not have any prior information about your organization. They might not know your mission. It's helpful to state your tagline, even if it is in the form of a hashtag.

- Use hashtags. I have used #feedthelowcountry for years. I like this because it accomplishes two things at once—it tells you our mission is to feed people, and it tells you where we are located. I also started using #kindnessarmy once I realized that's what we have become. Sometimes our events or posts are not directly about food—they may be about free laundry or one of our other community collaborations. I try to keep the hashtags uniform and not use full-sentence hashtags. No one can read full-sentence hashtags, and they are not widely followed.

- Bring in new followers with hashtags that are very general— things like #food, #donate, and #holiday are great ways to reach people who may have had no prior interest in your mission at all.

When used effectively, social media will bring awareness of your mission to folks you never expected to reach. You will hear from people all over the country and maybe even the world who are doing similar work, and you will be inspired by their different approaches. It has been vital to building and maintaining our Kindness Army.

Lighting a Spark with Kindness

Perhaps the best part of having this army of kind people is that they each have their own passions. For example, real estate agents are doing food drives and picking up donations from people's front porches. This fills the Boxes but also gives them a great networking opportunity. Their use of the Boxes as a means to network and drum up more business does not take away from the food that is going into the Boxes and subsequently into people's stomachs.

One of the most important realizations I have come to during the creation and rise of the Blessing Box Project is that you might never know the spark that you are lighting in others with your example of kindness.

Chapter 11: Free Laundry Events

Our vast group of volunteers extends into communities both near and far, into areas that are both heavily populated and rural, and it encompasses all ages and ethnic groups. After the Project picked up steam, I was inspired to branch out and become more involved within the communities our Boxes are serving. To this end, I launched a series of fundraising campaigns, which enabled us to host free laundry events.

The efforts were largely spearheaded by one of our most loyal volunteers, who likes to be called Lady C. Over time Lady C turned the laundry days into tiny festivals. She'd organize local restaurants and businesses to donate food, laundry supplies, and goodies to give away for attendees. She would put a small amount of cash in envelopes and have participants guess the amount, with the winner getting the envelope. At some point over the years, she acquired a microphone and a speaker that she now brings with her to the events, furthering her status as Master of Ceremonies. During the events, she makes live social media videos to encourage people to come help or to come wash their clothes for free. As I mentioned before, when you make events like that a party, people feel better about having to rely on the generosity of strangers to meet their basic needs.

The logistics of the events were very manageable. Essentially, we made a Facebook event page, and people donated money directly to the event through Facebook. We converted that money into rolls of quarters at our bank. Then our volunteers showed up at the laundromats, and we used the quarters to do laundry for everybody who came in until we ran out of quarters. We did at least one free laundry event every three to four months from the fall of 2017 until the pandemic began in 2020. When the pandemic started to subside, laundry days were the first thing we started planning again.

We never cared why the participants needed their laundry done, and we never asked about their circumstances. I think this is another great way to expand on anonymous giving: you need your laundry done, you come in, and we'll pay for it. It is also a great way to dignify low-income communities because paying for laundry is something everyone needs, and it is quite expensive. It's about $7 to wash just one load—and more to dry it. If you're a server who needs clean clothes for your job, that is a sizeable chunk of your income. We had senior citizens coming to wash their bed linens and curtains because doing so was a luxury that many had skipped over for a long time.

After we established a routine and rapport at the laundry facilities, we started bringing food to the events and donating laundry supplies like soap, hangers, new laundry baskets, and bags. These events were a great way to get to know the people our Boxes serve, but in a fun and friendly way that allowed them to remain dignified.

As the laundry events grew, businesses in the community started to take notice. We have a relationship with a local call center because they host a Box at their office, and when they found out about our free laundry days, they decided to sponsor a laundry day event with food, games, and giveaways. It was like a block party at the laundromat, just the way Lady C likes it. Over time, other

organizations asked to be part of our laundry day events—the folks who pass out naloxone in case of drug overdoses, the folks who hand out free condoms to prevent STDs, and even the folks who run blood drives. That relationship translated well during the coronavirus pandemic because blood donations became especially important, and the blood drive company offered COVID-19 antibody testing along with their standard monetary gift card for donors.

At one of our free laundry events, I met a young man. Let's call him David. David had recently undergone a very serious medical procedure and had a long recovery ahead of him. He lived near the laundromat and spent most of the day with us. Throughout the day he thanked all the volunteers for helping him. Once he and I spoke one-on-one, however, he explained that he was so glad we were there but not for him—for the elderly people of that community.

He told me about going to the home of an older woman whose laundry had piled up but who was physically unable to get it to us. David told me her house smelled because she had not washed clothes or linens in a while; she was on a fixed income, and laundry was a luxury she often could not afford. He helped her load the laundry in her car and stayed with her until she was done so he could help her get home. David says we gave his elderly friend a clean slate—a reset. David was emotional as he spoke about what it meant for people to give up their time and money to do this seemingly small act. He asked me to tell everyone how much it meant to his neighborhood that a tiny bit of the burden of daily life could be lifted.

I hope through our laundry days that we have inspired not just companies but also individuals to think of creative ways to do a little bit of good in the world. I want people to know that it doesn't have to be a grand gesture; you can go set $20 in quarters inside the laundromat, and that's going to help somebody get through the week. You can pay for the car behind you in the drive-through lane on your lunch break. Return someone's shopping cart to the appropriate place. Put money in an expired parking meter. Take pizza to the police station. Deliver flowers to the nursing home. Go out of your way to tell someone's boss what a good job their employee did. The possibilities for adding a little bit of good in the world are endless.

In the end, the idea of anonymous giving comes down to doing things for other people not because of who they are, but because of who you are.

Chapter 12: 2020—The Yearlong Empathy Test

The year 2020 was absolutely terrible, but when it was all said and done, I kind of miss it, and I would bet you do too. Hear me out.

You see, this Project has always been about finding common ground and what makes us the same rather than what makes us different. In 2020, the need for kindness and empathy was what the whole world needed more than just about anything. Everyone was struggling in some way, and we had to find ways to connect with each other while staying six feet apart.

When in our lifetimes have we ever had a common enemy like COVID-19? Everyone in the whole world was fighting the same global pandemic. Living through a pandemic meant that essentially you could have the same conversation with anyone on the earth along these lines:

You: "Well, I had planned to _____, but then, well, you know, COVID-19 happened."

Complete stranger: "Yeah, I understand. Me too."

We all had this conversation dozens of times. I knew before it was over that I would miss that common ground. I started to miss it as I heard and saw friends taking those first steps to bring us back to "normal." Don't get me wrong—I want everyone to be healthy and working, and for the kids to be playing sports, and to get back to a world where we aren't worried about how close we are standing next to each other. But for a brief moment in time, there was comfort in acknowledging that we were all suffering these unknown things together.

A Shift in Anonymous Giving

The COVID-19 pandemic irreversibly changed our Project. We added more than fifty-four locations from March to November of 2020 and had a resurgence of requests for media interviews. The interest piqued again because this type of anonymous giving is a great way to help someone without ever having to be physically near them. I'm glad that the network of Boxes and the general structure of the Lowcountry Blessing Box Project was in place before the pandemic happened. Organizations doing food giveaways and distributions started to follow our model and put the donations out on tables for people to come pick up.

One of our community resource centers asked me to convert newspaper distribution boxes so they could put them outside their building during this time, and we were able to make them six new Blessing Boxes very quickly thanks to our connections with the local paper. People who hadn't heard about anonymous giving got enthusiastically involved. Several churches moved their food pantries from inside the building to outside the building.

We have always taken donations of nonperishable items that are not foods, like diapers, school supplies, and pet food. These items were welcomed and embraced during the pandemic, especially soap and toilet paper—crazy to think that these essentials became coveted and hard to find! It was incredible to watch folks anonymously give those hard-to-find items, which many people were afraid to go to the store to look for, especially when it was sometimes unknown when the stores would restock certain essentials.

A New Meaning of Food Insecurity

During the coronavirus pandemic, everybody experienced some level of food insecurity. Some folks had the money to pay for things but were afraid to go to the store. That situation was not easy to process by people who were food secure before 2020. It was a new feeling to need something very basic like toilet paper but to be unable to access it. My hope is that previously food secure people who experienced a barrier between themselves and their lunch gained empathy and an understanding of the food insecure folks. Not only were many people living paycheck to paycheck before the pandemic, but many of them had their struggles deepened by job losses, lack of childcare, the pressure of homeschooling, and the general anxiety of staying healthy during a health crisis. The COVID-19 pandemic was an opportunity for us to further develop our sense of empathy for people who are food insecure.

Another interesting development toward the beginning of the pandemic was the appreciation people continuously expressed for the sense of connection they felt by using—both donating to and shopping at—the Blessing Boxes. I am sure the connection remained even after we all emerged from quarantine, but we were all so desperate for human interaction at that time that it came up frequently in emails and social media comments. Even though our donors don't know the recipients, their stories, or what's going on in their lives, they do know that the peanut butter they put in the Box on Monday is gone on Tuesday, so somebody needed it enough to come get it. Just knowing that other people were still out there in this small way seemed to be a comfort to people in our Kindness Army.

There seemed to also be a new respect for those in need. We saw an uptick in people leaving notes in the Boxes: sometimes thank-you notes or just cards from kids. The Boxes helped remind people that even though we exist in our separate realities, we are still connected as a community. Seeing a Blessing Box on your street reminds you that you are part of something larger and that your neighbors care about you and others.

The slogan we used throughout the pandemic was "Clean Hands. Open Hearts." This was intended to serve not only as the one-millionth daily reminder to wash your hands but also as a reminder that we operate under the idea of anonymous giving. Even if you were the one donating food back in January 2020 and now you've lost your job and need to feed your family—the Blessing Box is there for you too. There are no questions or judgments. Our hearts must remain open to one another in order for us to come together as a community and get through this ordeal. Clean hands alone are not enough. We must also keep open hearts.

Throughout the weeks of lockdowns, we saw an increase in publicity and an uptick in monetary donations. We were contacted by organizations that wanted to give us grants or route some of their own corporate money into our efforts. With so many resources at my disposal all of a sudden, I felt guilty that I was hunkered down at my house with my kids and not out in the community doing laundry events and food drives. I leaned heavily on grocery delivery drivers and online store orders to fill the Boxes, and in the end, I do think we successfully navigated the toughest parts of the pandemic by keeping most of our locations stocked and still not overly exposing ourselves or our volunteers to the virus.

Overall, COVID-19 opened up opportunities for more Blessing Boxes to be installed, and people responded in innovative ways. Following our lead on anonymous giving, a bar started putting food out on collapsible tables on their sidewalk, and churches used Blessing Boxes as a way of providing food in addition to their in-house pantries. I enjoyed watching as these new sources of anonymous giving made their way into the fray with fresh ideas on how to help people while remaining socially distant.

This Project was always meant to bridge gaps, but in 2020, gaps became caverns. Those who were on the margins before now qualified for assistance from food banks in huge numbers, and food banks were overwhelmed. Some former donors to our Boxes were now having to eat from them. One of the many lessons learned during the yearlong empathy test was that we are all connected, so we should all treat one another better.

Chapter 13: Raising Kind Kids

Teaching kids the value of serving others is on a lot of parents' to-do lists, but how and where do we fit that into everything else life throws our way? The virtues of kindness, tolerance, and empathy are so important to instill in our youth, and this Project aims to make that a little easier. You and your children can do good deeds together right in your neighborhood.

The simple concept of leave what you can, take what you need is something kids can understand. Understanding why people need access to food while keeping their dignity, however, is a bit tougher. The Blessing Box Project tries not to place a value or judgment on another person's struggles. The Boxes are intended to help folks who are food insecure, like the family who has an unexpected medical bill or the young person working two jobs and experiencing a major car problem. Kids can understand that unexpected things happen, and also that bad things happen to good people. They can probably recall a time in their lives that they needed a little help but were too embarrassed to ask or weren't sure where to turn for assistance.

My sister has three children under the age of ten and is passionate about raising kind kids. She tried to find places in her community where her children would be able to volunteer but really struggled due to their ages. Lack of opportunities for hands-on experiences was one of her motivators for beginning a Blessing Box Project in her town.

Here in Charleston, there are very few organizations that provide volunteer opportunities for kids. I was thrilled to find the organization I Heart Hungry Kids,[1] a nonprofit that works to fight childhood hunger in the Charleston community, when my girls were small. My kids loved volunteering at the food bank to pack bags of food at the I Heart Hungry Kids packing parties and getting to know the kids who founded the organization. This relationship later grew into a partnership with the Blessing Box Project when we started exploring the issue of school lunch debt.

Early in the Project, I was asked to speak to a class of third graders about food insecurity and food deserts. The teachers had introduced the idea to the students and asked me to talk about how our Project gives real-world relief to this somewhat abstract problem. Kids seem to grasp the idea that we should give to others without expecting anything in return—not for praise or attention or to brag about it on social media. We should do it just because it is the right thing to do. When you have more than you need, you should build a longer table, not a higher fence. This is more challenging for adults to accept than for kids. Kids are not inherently judgmental. They do not think less of people who have less. That is something society teaches them later.

In that third-grade class was a little girl named Merritt. Merritt came home from school and insisted to her parents that she create a Blessing Box near their house. Her parents were supportive and obtained a newspaper dispenser that they upcycled into an adorable green-and-blue Blessing Box for their front yard. Their area is much more rural that other parts of the Lowcountry, and part of Merritt's motivation was the realization that she lived in a food desert.

As if this were not sweet enough, the story gets better. Around that time, I was unavailable to appear on a television interview for World Kindness Day, so I asked Merritt to step in for me—and she did a magnificent job. Her Box was up and running and feeding

---

[1] Learn more about I Heart Hungry Kids at www.ihearthungrykids.org.

people in her hometown, and we discovered that she was a natural on TV to boot! Merritt's school also installed a Blessing Box on their campus.

Two years later, the same teacher asked me to speak to her first graders. I asked Merritt's mom if she would again be willing to stand in for me and she obliged. I was so touched and proud to receive photos of then fifth-grade Merritt speaking to a group of intent six-year-olds at her school as she told them her story about creating her Blessing Box and being part of the solution to food insecurity in her community. This felt like a watershed moment, a changing of the guard of sorts. The next generation of Kindness Army participants was already up and running.

One of our hosts' children started Art in the Park at the Snack Shack—a project that was awarded a Disney Be Inspired grant. They set up their Snack Shack, a wagon that functions as a mobile food pantry, in downtown parks along with art supplies and invited other kids to join them in crafting, playing, eating, and enjoying the outdoors. They used the Blessing Box concept of working to end hunger while having fun. The kids who came out to do crafts were given snacks while they worked and also bags of food to take home with them at the end.

Over the years several Blessing Boxes have been built by scout troops, civic youth organizations, and religious youth groups. Two women who ran a summer camp for kids added a Box to their community as part of a project with their campers. One Box was built by kids at Vacation Bible School. With more than two hundred locations, it is hard to list all the connections to kids' involvement, but getting children involved in helping others has undoubtedly been a part of our passion as well as our success.

My Own (Hopefully) Kind Kids

My kids assist at many of the events that the Blessing Box Project either runs or helps other organizations within the community. I had a chat with them after we gave away hundreds of frozen turkeys, socks, and warm clothing for a Thanksgiving donation drive-through. I thanked them for helping and asked if they knew that they were part of making other families' holidays better. We talked about how not everyone has everything they need, like a safe, warm home and enough food to eat. We talked about how it would feel to be hungry on Thanksgiving or to not have family to gather with. Because we had had similar conversations before, the kids were not surprised by any of my questions or comments, but I was surprised by theirs.

They said that their contributions did not really make a difference because they only helped get the balloon decorations together and hang up signs. I explained to them that sometimes it is hard to ask for help when you need it, and it can be especially hard for grown-ups to ask for help to feed or clothe their families. By making a turkey giveaway into a "party" atmosphere (this one had been carnival themed), they helped make it easier for the grown-ups to be there receiving assistance. Sometimes the people who need help look like they have everything together and are doing just fine. It is those people, I think, that struggle the most to accept assistance. But if you can make a turkey donation drive-through look like a carnival, accepting a "handout" becomes more tolerable.

I recently found several rolls of quarters that had probably rolled around under the passenger seat of my car for months, and I decided to package them up to distribute at our local laundromat. I divided them into baggies and took my youngest with me. Six-year-olds have absolutely no hesitation walking up to strangers, handing them a bag of quarters, and walking away. While that might have been awkward for me as an adult, my daughter did not think twice. Plus, it makes the laundromat patrons feel less uncomfortable accepting such a surprise gift when it comes from a bouncing little human than a fellow adult.

When I started the Blessing Box Project, I was so motivated to bring the community together that I did not fully think of how creating something like this would impact my own kids. I have always been moved to be a helper, and I think part of me assumed my offspring would be as well. I want to be a good example for them both as a citizen and as a mom. I want them to feel empowered to make change and to stand up to injustice. When my kids see my interviews, they think you can be "famous" and be on TV for being kind to people. We have more work to do, but this is a good start.

Ideas for Getting Your Kids Involved

Here are a few easy ways to get your kids involved in giving:

- Ask your kids what kinds of things they think might be useful to place inside the Blessing Box that can help a family get through until payday—for example, canned soups and fruits, peanut butter, pasta, rice, and other staples. Baby wipes, diapers, pet food, and travel-size shampoo and toothpaste are also helpful. School supplies, bottled water, sunscreen, and coffee are some unexpected but always appreciated donations too. Undoubtedly, your kids will have more ideas of things they believe would be helpful.

- Let them pick out donations. Getting the kids involved is as easy as taking them to the grocery store and letting them pick out a few items to donate, then driving them to a Blessing Box near you. You may want to encourage older kids to earn the money to buy their donations and make it a monthly project.

- Get them involved in themed events. As I mentioned earlier, a few times a year we promote themed donations like back-to-school supplies, Thanksgiving meals in individual bags, and boxes of Valentine cards. We also give prizes for decorating neighborhood Boxes for St. Patrick's Day and Halloween. During the holiday season, we encourage donors to add one food item a day to a Box for the month of December, like a reverse Advent calendar, or to collect it all month and then donate it to the Box on Christmas. Kids love the holiday decorations and are so creative with their ideas. They also love looking for themed items to put in the Boxes. It's amazing how many orange-and-black-labeled foods they can find in the grocery store when they're looking!

- Create a scavenger hunt. One mom who follows our social media invented a scavenger hunt game for her kids. She printed our Blessing Box map and had them circle which Boxes they wanted to "find," and then they set off around town with donations to fill the selected locations' Boxes.

- Encourage your kids to ask for donations in place of gifts. Several times a year, we receive photos from kids who asked for nonperishable food donations instead of birthday gifts. What a heartwarming way to give up gifts on their special day. My own kids haven't yet achieved this level of selflessness, but we are working on it.

- Volunteer with your kids. My own kids have been involved with the Project by helping decorate for events and through other ways that help recipients feel more dignified in accepting help. Prepandemic, the Project was involved in a program through Disney that encourages kids and families to volunteer together. We had a series of events planned that included free laundry events and packing parties to make meal bags for our Blessing Boxes. Disney gives away park tickets to organizations that promote kid-volunteerism.

Once you get your kids to start thinking about how they can spread kindness by giving back to their community, you might be surprised at their creativity. For example, older kids might sponsor food drives to fulfill school service hour requirements or build a Box as an Eagle Scout Project. The possibilities for involvement are endless. As I learned as a teenager in Appalachia, kids really can change their communities, and they need not wait around for adults to lead the way. A good idea is a good idea, regardless of the age of the person who hatched it.

Chapter 14: Catch Up on Lunch

In December of 2018, I started receiving messages from military families and civilian government employees about a potential federal government shutdown and not knowing when federal employees would be paid. The Charleston area is home to many individuals and families whose livelihoods depends on paychecks from the federal government. Because the branches of our government could not agree on how to fund the functions of the government, it was shutdown for 35 days. During that time, the employees were either sent home or worked without pay and their number one concern was providing for their families. Specifically, I was receiving messages asking for my help with paying for their kids' school lunches.

I had never before considered the problem of school lunch debt. Once I had received the messages from the military families, I posted on the Blessing Box social media pages asking others to share their experiences. I learned that often kids aren't allowed to go on field trips or participate in other fun activities when their parents owe money for their lunches. Schools withhold report cards, and some even deny the children food if their debts are over a certain amount.

Here are some excerpts from messages I received:

- "My daughter gets food stamps. She is a single parent and rarely gets child support. I help her as much as I can. She signed my grands up for free lunch and her application got lost. The school wants my daughter to pay for the time that her application was lost before she got approved. It's a couple hundred dollars. She will try to pay it from her tax return. The kids have always gotten free lunch, the problem happened when they switched schools and moved between counties this year."

- "I've had this issue with my son when money is tight. I just try to send him to school with a good breakfast eaten before and a snack to eat during the day. Still isn't enough when they don't get home until supper time!"

- "My daughter bought milk and ice cream without letting us know (we pack her lunch) every day for a whole semester before we got a bill or a phone call. By that time, we already had a huge bill."

With more research, I learned that some school districts also send the lunch debts to collection agencies. What a terrible position for a child! As if the children have control over their parents' finances! I was incensed and knew the Kindness Army had to do something.

I mentioned the issue to a friend of mine whose family is in the restaurant business. She was also motivated to do something, but we were not sure where to start. Over time, the issue came up with another friend who runs I Heart Hungry Kids, the nonprofit organization I mentioned that is dedicated to kids helping to feed other kids. This seemed like a perfect time for the three of us to collaborate, and thus Catch Up on Lunch was born. I both came up with the name and insisted that it was far too cheesy for us to actually use. I was overruled.

The more we learned about school lunch debt, the more determined we became to both shine a light on this problem and try to make a dent in our local school kids' debts. We learned the term "lunch shaming" and became familiar with the legislative and policy debates raging around the country surrounding school lunch debt. For example, California has a law that says all kids get to eat school lunch even if they don't have money with them to pay for it. Other states have gone the opposite way and have cafeteria workers stamp kids' hands marking them as unable to pay or refuse to serve them when they cannot pay.[2]

In most school districts, students are screened to see if their families qualify for either free or reduced-price lunches. We found that many families do not fill out this paperwork— they don't think they qualify, or their students simply don't bring the forms home, or they are embarrassed to ask for help. We also found that some students have a more complicated reason for not completing the free lunch form—often literacy, language barriers, or custody issues can play a part in not receiving the aid they qualify for. This contributes to lunch debts at schools and ongoing financial hardships at home.

In 2019, 75 percent of school districts reported having school lunch debt.[3] Kids who are hungry can't focus on learning. Schools are forced to choose between incurring the debt or feeding their students. Since hungry students are unable to focus on their studies, most schools give meals to students with past-due balances.

Large past-due lunch balances take funds from staff development, learning materials, arts programs, and other initiatives in our schools. It also places students at risk for lunch shaming, a practice in which students who have used up their school meal accounts are denied lunches, served cold or cheap food instead of a hot meal, or are sent home with stamps on their hands to

---

[2] Crystal FitzSimons, "School Lunch Debt and Lunch Shaming Is a Problem That Needs a National Solution," October 16, 2019, https://www.nbcnews.com/think/opinion/school-lunch-debt-lunch-shaming-problem-needs-national-solution-ncna1066461.

[3] Michelle Lou, "75% of US School Districts Report Student Meal Debt. Here's What They're Doing to Combat the Problem," CNN, May 17, 2019, https://www.cnn.com/2019/05/17/us/unpaid-school-lunch-debt-trnd/index.html.

remind their parents or guardians to settle their balances. In years past, celebrities and various corporations have made headlines by paying off kids' school lunch debts. Catch Up on Lunch intended to do the same.

Spirit Nights and Other Fundraisers

We started addressing the lunch debt problem by asking restaurants to host Spirit Nights, in which a portion of the night's proceeds are donated to our cause. We took direct donations and did several interviews. We visited local civic organizations and spoke out on social media about kids having to suffer and be embarrassed because their parents or guardians either hadn't filled out the forms to obtain free lunch when they qualified for that assistance or had not paid for their school lunches for another reason.

In our first year, we paid off more than $25,000 in school lunch debt—which covered only four schools. I am still shocked that $25,000 covered the debt at so few schools. In other areas of the country, that amount would have covered the debt for entire school districts or even the entire state. In our tri-county area, the total debt was somewhere around $300,000. This indicated multiple failings on a few different fronts. School lunches are about $2 to $3 each, so several hundred thousand dollars total is inexcusable.

During our second school year with the Catch Up on Lunch program, we had a head start and were feeling good about our ability to repeat our fundraising effort. We were chosen to be the charity for a very cool event called Hope on Goat, which takes place on Goat Island near Charleston, South Carolina. On leap day of 2020, the Hope on Goat oyster roast, bluegrass festival, and silent auction was a huge success. We had a great time and raised a significant amount of money to help pay off Lowcountry families' lunch debts.

However, the world seemingly came to a halt shortly thereafter due to the pandemic, so we weren't able to finalize our plans to repay the lunch debt. Eventually, it became clear that no one was going back to school in person for quite some time.

In the fall of 2020 when school resumed, all students were offered free lunch at all Charleston area local schools regardless of their ability to pay. Even kids who were doing school virtually at home were able to pick up breakfast and lunch every school day at no charge. Whether our efforts had anything to do with this policy, we will never know, and only time will tell whether this policy will continue once the schools return to some semblance of normal—or whether Catch Up on Lunch will come into play again. It is my hope that the "new normal" does not include shaming children for their parents' financial situations.

Chapter 15: Fresh Takes on Free Pantries

One of the most rewarding aspects of founding the Blessing Box Project and growing the Kindness Army has been watching others put their own personal spins on the idea of anonymous giving, whether inspired by our Project or by other broader anonymous giving movements. I pointed out the running club whose members "ruck" with backpacks full of cans to fill Boxes along their running route, as well as the Free Fridge movement in larger cities with artists who turn the refrigerators into art that feeds people. Many other times, the spin has involved the donation of nonfood items. These fresh takes on the idea of a free food pantry are all brilliant, with each one more creative than the next.

Here are ten of the most popular nonfood donation ideas.

1.   Diapers

Early in the Project, I was connected with one of our local diaper banks. Bundles of Joy – Diaper Bank of the Lowcountry[4] gives away diapers to those in need—not anonymously, but in a very organic, pop-up sort of manner similar to our Boxes. We brainstormed but were unable to come up with a way to make sure that the diapers people donated in our Boxes were going to the clients who had registered with the diaper bank for assistance. It was complicated because of the diapers' sizing and the changing needs of a family over time.

---

[4] Learn more about Bundles of Joy – Diaper Bank of the Lowcountry at www.bundlesofjoydiaperbank.org.

So I started generally encouraging the donation of diapers as well as baby wipes and formula in the Blessing Boxes and received a great response. Depending on the location, some of the Boxes are flush with baby items all the time. My local Box is in an area with tons of families, and I see baby products in it nearly every time I visit. I also see posts in parent-centric social media groups that either remind parents to donate diapers or announce specific items they saw—"Size 5 Pull-Ups in the Blessing Box in case anyone is in need." It warms my heart to see this because it really feels like the community is rallying around one another in a very useful and tangible way.

2.   Pet Food

Some people's babies are furrier than the kind of babies who wear diapers, and those fur babies are taken care of by our Blessing Boxes, too. In fact, in the fall of 2020, we launched our very first pet-food-only Blessing Box at a business that caters exclusively to pets. I have learned over the course of this adventure that those who are suffering through some of the most intense food security issues often feed their animals before they feed themselves. For that reason, and because I also love my dogs, I have encouraged the donations of dog, cat, and other pet foods in our Boxes.

I do make an exception to the rule against donating open food when it is pet food. Most of us have experienced the predicament of buying a food that our dog won't eat or is allergic to—and donating it to a Blessing Box seems like a good solution in that scenario. I also donated my dog's food supply after he passed away, and it gave me some peace to know it was going to help another dog somewhere.

The response is always positive to my pet food donation requests, and—bonus—it gives me an excuse to share pictures of my own pets!

3. Toiletries

From the inception of the Project, I have also encouraged toiletry donations. This began by asking people to save their hotel-size products for our Boxes after they traveled. It evolved into encouraging toothpaste and toothbrush donations during National Dental Hygiene Month (which is in October to coincide with Halloween!). Around the holidays, I make social media posts telling people to donate any unneeded or unwanted lotion sets or bath products they received for Christmas. Nearly all toiletries are nonperishable and are needed, whether it be shampoo, soap, deodorant, or even personal care items like tampons.

4. Feminine Hygiene Products

The Homeless Period Project[5] is a fantastic organization whose involvement in our Project has really taken us to the next level for

---

[5] Learn more about the Homeless Period Project at www.homelessperiodproject.org.

being able to provide access to personal hygiene items. Our local chapter was able to assign a volunteer to each of our Blessing Box locations—that's more than two hundred different places—to routinely stock pads and tampons in our Boxes. This is in addition to the organization's work in local schools to provide period products to students and their dedication to the homeless population, including donations to shelters. Like us, their work is accessed not only by the homeless community but also by a cross section of the community that lacks secure resources to purchase these items on their own.

Women and girls are missing school and work because they do not have adequate products during their periods, which is why we encourage donations of feminine hygiene items in our Boxes from those not involved with the Homeless Period Project as well. If you're wondering what you should donate to your local women's shelter, consider giving them period products. Lack of access to these products is a healthcare issue and one that deserves more attention in our communities.

5.   Socks

Another item that is highly sought after but often overlooked at shelters is socks. For Christmas in 2018, my mom bought each member of my immediate family (all seventeen of us) a pair of socks. At our house, the youngest person opens gifts first. That was my then four-year-old nephew. When he opened his socks, he took one look at them, said, "Aww, socks!" and tossed them on the floor. We had a good laugh because it was pretty typical—not many four-year-olds are excited to receive socks.

Next up was my daughter, also four, who, having seen the reaction her cousin got from his socks comment, did the same thing—"Aww, socks!"

And so it began. One by one we opened our socks, and one by one we tossed them on the ground with a laugh. It became and remains a running family joke. But these weren't just any socks. My mom had learned about Bombas, a company that donates a pair of socks for each pair that they sell.[6] So by purchasing all of us this not-so-exciting gift, my mom had caused seventeen pairs of socks to be donated to homeless shelters or other nonprofits.

Shortly thereafter, I applied for the Blessing Boxes to be one of the distribution locations for the donated socks, and my request was granted. I normally discourage clothing donations in the Blessing Boxes; if clothing were allowed, people would bring *all* their clothing donations and the Boxes, which are not very big to begin with, would end up stuffed full of clothing with no room remaining for food. Socks, however, are such a needed item and are small, so we allow this exception to the rule.

We have been blessed to receive an annual shipment from Bombas. Some socks go into the Blessing Boxes, and the majority are given away at our other events like free laundry days or turkey giveaway days. We also distribute them to help our various community partners, like events at our local retirement home or in hygiene kits given to teenagers at the alternative high school.

6. Plants

We have a Blessing Box near a community library, and after several years, the hosts decided to add an extra element—they built a shelving unit and painted it with the words "Give a plant, take a plant." I have been accused of many things, but never of having a green thumb. The idea that one could keep something alive long enough to pass it along to someone else is foreign to me. However,

---

[6] Learn more about Bombas at www.bombas.com.

the plant exchange has caught on, and many folks in the community are enjoying this exchange of fragile live beings. Folks donate dozens of tomato plants at a time, and the plants find their ways into new homes, yards, and gardens.

7.   Natural Disaster Preparedness

Here in Charleston, we have had named storms nearly every year for the past five years. Living on the coast gives you no choice but to expect the worst during hurricane season. And while that is true in our area for hurricanes, it is likely also true for other types of natural disasters in other parts of the country and the world.

Regardless of our type of storm—snowstorms, wildfires, hurricanes—very often the people who are least able to prepare end up being the ones who are hit the hardest. When the city closes down or issues evacuation warnings, hourly workers are the first to lose wages. The longer things stay closed, the more money they are losing from their paychecks. For storms where evacuations are ordered, those with limited resources are not able to pack their cars and head inland to a hotel for a week. If they have a car, they may not have gas money, and if they have gas money, they may not have hotel money, and if they have hotel money, they might not have rent money next month, because they did not work for a week while they were evacuated. It is a vicious cycle and a choice between their safety and their financial stability.

At the start of hurricane season, all the local media outlets will start encouraging people to get their hurricane kits and plans in order to prepare. I also encourage people to pick up extra provisions to donate to the Blessing Boxes when they are doing their own hurricane preseason shopping. Batteries, canned food, bottled water, garbage bags, first aid kits, manual can openers, and other basic disaster supplies are all great donations to a Blessing Box because they are all nonperishable.

The typical cycle for us coast dwellers is as follows: keep an eye on the storm, assess the likelihood it will come our way, stock up on food and water, wait it out, and then repeat for each storm. I have been encouraging two steps to be added to the hurricane prep process—(1) buy extra supplies to donate to the Blessing Boxes before the storms, and (2) once the storm has passed, donate what you didn't use to the Boxes for someone in need. Hopefully, these habits will catch on because the storms certainly have shown no signs of stopping anytime soon.

Hurricanes and other natural disasters are the types of events that convert food secure households into households that need the assistance of the Blessing Boxes. Lost days at work, damage to the house, flooded-out cars, and other unfortunate circumstances take a toll on a monthly budget but often do not qualify the household for other types of aid due to the employment status of the adults living there.

8. Prayer Intention Box

One of the churches that hosts a Blessing Box has added a small compartment on the side of their Box that resembles a suggestion box, similar to one you might see at a business. It is locked and has a small slit at the top for papers to be slid in, but it is not large enough for anything else. It is a Prayer Intention Box.

The pastor of the church keeps the key and is the only one with access to the intentions once they are placed in the prayer box. I love the creativity and the motivation behind this idea. While this Project is not associated with any one religion or belief system, should someone feel inclined to request prayers for their particular intention, I think this is a brilliant way to do it and a great addition to the direct purposes of the Blessing Box itself. As another bonus, I think it blurs the lines on the reasons why someone may be visiting the Box. If someone in need was hesitant to be seen there, they might tell themselves or others that they were just stopping by to add a prayer intention.

Naming the Project the Blessing Box had less to do with my own religious beliefs than it did with my enjoyment of alliteration and the fact that here in the South, everyone likes to say "have a blessed day." Those who know me will tell you that I avoid talking about religion most of the time, and I think faith should, generally, be very personal. However, I did learn many years ago in the hills of Appalachia that putting religion into practice is an important part of my own personal faith.

The Blessing Boxes are at Catholic, Methodist, African Methodist Episcopal, and Baptist churches, at mosques, and at the homes of Jewish people and atheists. One of my favorite things about the concept of anonymous giving through free pantries is that everyone has to eat. When I was asked to be the speaker at the Medical University of South Carolina for their observation of Martin Luther King, Jr., Day, I was honored to speak about the Blessing Box Project around that theme—everyone eats. No matter who you are, what you believe, or where you want to go, you need to have food to do it, and food is too often a privilege.

9.   The Giving Fence

In colder areas, I have seen the implementation of the Giving Fence, where coats, hats, and gloves are hung for anyone in need to take. We have not done this in Charleston, mostly because there is not a ton of need for a winter coat here. However, we have assisted some of our community partners in coat drives and also sponsored free laundry events just for coats to be given away to the homeless community. I wanted to mention it here for anyone who may live in colder or snowy climates because it's a great way to give back—

especially in the days of COVID-19, when contactless giving is so much more important than before.

10. Book Drives and Book Fairs

This tenth and final fresh take on the free pantry movement is a little different. The original Little Free Pantry, which inspired me, was itself inspired by the Little Free Library. The fresh take on the Little Free Library that I have been promoting over the years has two fronts—one as book drives through online shopping and anonymous donation to various community partners, and the other by encouraging our supporters to send extra money to their kids' or grandkids' teachers during annual book fairs to pay for the kids whose parents either forgot or were unable to send money for them to buy books. Anonymously, of course, because sneaky kindness is the best.

- Community partners—We have leveraged the power of the Kindness Army to buy lots of books for kids who are part of the various community resource centers where we either have Blessing Boxes or otherwise have connections. We have done this mainly by creating wish lists on Amazon and publicizing the links for our supporters to do their own shopping.

  The wish lists are a collaboration between the community centers and me. Several of the community partners serve kids of color almost exclusively and requested the lists to include books with protagonists who look like the kids they serve. Creating the book wish lists is quite a walk down memory lane for me because I get to add many of my favorite childhood books, along with books I love to read with my own kids. As an added perk, by creating and adding to these shopping lists, I also discover new books for my family.

The books from these wish lists do not go in the Blessing Boxes but either directly to the kids served at the community learning centers or into a Little Free Library at one of the laundromats where we do free laundry events. As I started creating the book lists, I could feel myself harken back to the days when my elementary teachers let us trick-or-treat for UNICEF and that motivation I had to make sure every single kid would be taken care of through my efforts.

- School book fairs—It's hard for me to imagine a worse feeling than being eight years old and having to watch your friends buy new books while you can't get anything because your parents can't afford that extra purchase.

  You might assume that your kids or grandkids are not in class with anyone who needs $10 for the book fair. I would caution you to reevaluate that assumption. People who are in need very often get good at blending in to look like they have it all under control. You might not have any idea who those kids are, but I would be willing to bet their teachers do.

  Like food, having books of their own is too often a privilege for kids when it should not be. And consider what it was like for the kids who were cut off from their access to books during the pandemic when schools and libraries were closed.

These fresh takes on the concept of the Little Free Pantry have been an incredibly rewarding and unexpected result of the growth and development of my Project from a little idea into a movement of kind people.

Chapter 16: The Angel Alliance

As the Project evolved and the Kindness Army grew, I received a most precious gift—the gift of a community of like-minded people who support me and my Project's mission.

In the fall of 2018, I received a phone call from a random number that I almost did not answer. Luckily, I picked up because the caller wanted to tell me that I was a finalist for an award, and the awards would be given at a black-tie event just after Thanksgiving.

I struggled to explain that while I was honored anyone would consider me for an award, the Blessing Box Project was meant to be anonymous. Showing up in a ball gown to potentially get a trophy was the opposite of that vision. The kindest, most soothing voice on the phone told me that someone had to be the face of this effort. Someone had to tell the world what this Kindness Army was up to— the lives they were impacting, the inspiration people were finding at these small wooden boxes, and that someone was me.

So I accepted and said I would be there. A million questions followed—mostly from my mom. I shared with her everything I knew at the time, which was not much. A family-owned grocery store wanted to recognize the "Angels" of the community and have a celebration of all the good things happening in our city. The business owners also wanted to honor the victims of the tragedy at Mother Emanuel AME Church, their families, and the survivors of the racially motivated mass shooting, and creating this award ceremony was a way to bring those goals together. The creators of the awards wanted to make sure that the Angels of the community were "getting their flowers" when still on Earth and wanted to give the families of the victims and survivors an opportunity to celebrate the legacies of their loved ones.

There would be eighteen finalists and nine awards given during a glamorous event with dinner and entertainment at a ballroom downtown. The nine awards would each be named for one of the people who perished at the hands of a white supremacist at the church that terrible night in June 2015. All the families of the victims would be present as well as the survivors.

All eighteen finalists were invited to attend a photo shoot and meet one another before the event. I was excited and nervous and curious. I knew only one of the finalists—she hosted a Blessing Box at her house in addition to being involved in many other community activities. Everyone else was a stranger to me. There was an older gentleman who had coached high school basketball for many years, a philanthropist who had championed many causes over the years, a young woman who organized huge events including a prom for kids at the alternative high school, and many others. Each of them, I would come to realize, had a heart that sought to serve others. As cheesy as it may sound, in this room of eighteen people who looked nothing alike, all of us were the same on the inside. This was the first official meeting of the Angel Alliance.[1]

On the night of the awards, my parents, four of my best friends, and three Blessing Box hosts and their families accompanied me and my husband. The ballroom was packed, and the energy was high. All of the finalists and our guests walked the red carpet still with no idea what exactly to expect of the evening. I had been so touched by the grace shown by the victims' families throughout the trial and events that followed the tragedy that I was not sure I was worthy to share the room with all of them. Because of the enormity and shock of the crime, the loss and the impact, everyone in Charleston had followed the aftermath closely. Being in the legal community and personally knowing many of the lawyers involved

---

[1] Learn more about the Angel Alliance at www.theangelalliance.com.

in the criminal proceedings, I had followed it even more closely than perhaps others.

My husband and I were seated with three other "Angels" and their guests. The night included praise dancers, a speech from the mayor, a visit from a radio personality from Anguilla, a poetry reading, and more. Throughout the event, the masters of ceremonies would pause and say to the finalists, "Angels, you know we love you—and that's why we are giving you . . ." and then a young man in a bow tie would deliver a small gift to each of us—a free oil change, a photography session, and other tokens.

Each award presentation was accompanied by a video from the victim's loved ones talking about their lives, their passions, and how much they were missed. I was given the last award of the night, named in honor of Ms. Myra Thompson. Ms. Thompson was a mother, wife, teacher, and so much more before her life was so needlessly taken.

I want to share my acceptance speech because writing this speech was the first time I publicly acknowledged what I had been quietly building for more than a year at that point, a Kindness Army.

Thank you to everyone who had a hand in planning this incredible evening. I am honored to be here tonight representing the thousands of anonymous people who make the Blessing Boxes project a reality. Blessing Boxes are anonymous donation sites for nonperishable food. We have one principle: leave what you can, take what you need.

I want to thank our board members, who have been with me since the first day I started building Blessing Boxes in my garage in early 2017. They have gone all in on this effort since that time, and some of their children have even been recognized by Disney for the work they do in our communities with their Snack Shack—a spin-off of the Blessing Box Project.

After I built the first four Blessing Boxes, I did what all the sane people do and connected with complete strangers on the internet. Those strangers became my people. People with hearts just like mine. People for whom I am so grateful. Many of them are here tonight. We started doing free laundry days and other community projects. Soon our project expanded.

Together we began building an army of kind people in Charleston. Currently, there are fifty-two locations where people can anonymously give or receive food throughout the Lowcountry.

I am truly humbled to be here amongst all of you incredible souls. On a personal note, I have a few people to thank. I want to thank my parents for being great role models for me, for encouraging me to seek justice in the world, whether that's food justice as I do with this Project or justice in the courtroom, which is what I do as my day job.

I've been practicing law in Charleston for eleven years. I've spent countless hours in trials and at hearings, and I've met thousands of people on their absolute worst days, but I have never witnessed the unshakable grace that was shown by all of these families throughout the tragic events at Mother Emanuel and afterward. What a testimony you all are to your loved ones. I pray we can all find just a shred of your dignity, for if we can, then the world might just be all right.

Finally, I want to thank my husband for supporting my crazy ideas, for lifting the heavy stuff, for being the best dad to our girls, and for being a great partner.

I created the Blessing Box Project on the heels of a heated election and in a divisive political climate to have something we can all agree on—that we should all be kinder to one another. Thank you for recognizing us.

In the weeks and months after the awards, I continued to connect with the other Angels, and we began doing more outreach efforts together—more food giveaways, more laundry events—and I gained more connections and soldiers for the Kindness Army. Today, the members of the Angel Alliance—which adds to its number each year—are some of our most integral community partners. We are all doing similar work, so we might as well do it together.

Chapter 17: Cultivating Your Kindness Army

When accepting the award for 2017 CNN Hero of the Year for her work in advocating for disabled people, the founder of Bitty and Beau's Coffee, Amy Wright, spoke directly to her children. She said, "I would not change you for the world, but I will change the world for you."[1] Bitty and Beau were both born with down syndrome, and their mother created a thriving coffee shop business that employs people with intellectual and developmental disabilities.[2] Her statement really hit home for me.

My own kids were not my primary focus when the Blessing Box Project came to fruition. They were still quite small and not ready to start volunteering. However, as my kids and the project grew, I realized the usefulness of the Boxes as a teaching tool to build empathy.

Is it not our job as parents try to better the world for our kids? I want my kids to live in a community of people that support each other regardless of political beliefs, race, religion, or gender. I want to change our little corner of the world, even if it is just ever so slightly, to make it kinder. And I want my kids to know that they – even as kids – have the power to help make that change.

---

[1] Melonyce McAfee, "Advocate for Disabled Workers is CNN 2017 Hero of the Year," CNN, March 8, 2018, https://www.cnn.com/2017/12/17/world/amy-wright-2017-cnn-hero-of-the-year.

[2] Learn more about Bitty and Beau's Coffee at www.bittyandbeauscoffee.com.

The Blessing Box Project has already achieved more than I could have ever imagined back in early 2017. The growth of this organization has always been organic, and I've tried to roll with the opportunities and collaborations that have presented themselves. I never had a grand plan or a goal that when objectively met, I will feel like it is time to bring this chapter of my life to a close. The hardest interview questions I get are about the future of the project and where we go from here. I don't know because it is not mine to control. I'm just pedaling the bike – the community at large is steering the project.

I have been given accolades for creating the Blessing Box Project, and news outlets have enjoyed running uplifting stories on it. However, stories about people like me and efforts like this are not the answer to ending food insecurity. Systematic and systemic change are the real answer to this complex problem. Blessing Boxes are a temporary fix; a momentary relief for a lot of people, but not enough to bring about the changes needed in our food systems to ensure that all people have access to a sustainable amount of healthy food. Archbishop Desmond Tutu has been attributed to saying, "There comes a time when we need to stop pulling people out of the river. We need to go upstream and find out why they are falling in." As we celebrate the success of the anonymous giving movement and talk about how we got to this point, let us not miss that now is that time to go upstream.

From Five to Two Hundred

In 2017, I thought it would be great to have a small network of Boxes throughout the county. I had my heart set on a dozen because that would cover most of the areas that I traveled to for work at the time. After I built the first four, we added five more in just about a month—in fact, it was so fast that I could not even tell you which location was number ten. Once the idea caught on, it seemed that a

new one popped up at least once a week for the next several months.

I did have a special plan in mind for when we got to number one hundred. I wanted to hold a dedication ceremony and name the Box in honor of someone, but Box one hundred also happened too fast for my plan to come to fruition. We did, however, do a one-hundred-can challenge in honor of the one hundredth Box becoming active. I challenged one hundred people to donate one hundred cans of food during the month of November 2019, a well-received idea particularly because it came just in time for the food holidays of Thanksgiving, Christmas, Hanukkah, and Kwanzaa. I do not think the hosts knew their Box was a milestone for the Project as a whole, but they held their own dedication ceremony at the AME Church where the Box was located and placed a big pink bow around it. I couldn't make it across town to see the Box for several months, so I was very grateful for their festive photo!

The 150th Blessing Box was placed during the coronavirus pandemic to honor a frontline medical worker who was retiring. Her coworkers had built and installed the Blessing Box as a surprise. Not only was this a milestone because it was number 150, but what a fitting tribute to someone who had dedicated herself and her career to care for others—and in a global pandemic too! The 150th Box, located on Hilton Head Island, the furthermost point of the South Carolina Lowcountry before the Georgia state line, also fulfilled one of my initial goals for the Project—to expand to Hilton Head Island, Beaufort, Bluffton, and other areas in the southern part of the Lowcountry.

We recently added the two hundredth Blessing Box to our map, and although the pandemic gave me time to plan something special, I didn't have the wherewithal to be out in public to see it through. Making plans is so 2019 anyway. The 210th Box was added before I even had time to lament that we did not formally celebrate the two-hundredth one! The new trend is to add more Free Community Fridges to the existing network of Boxes.

Past and Future Goals

Once the Project started gaining traction, I set a goal to have coverage in each of our local media outlets—both print and television. I also did several web-based talk shows to promote the Project. Nearly all the interviews I have done over the course of the Project have been after a journalist heard about what I had created, not because I reached out to ask to be interviewed. I believe I have now checked all the boxes of appearing on each of our local media outlets.

If I had it to do again, I would not be so coy when it came to the media. I largely sat back and waited for journalists to ask me to give an interview or be a guest on their show. I have learned that "feel-good stories" are always needed, and it is ok to reach out with press releases or requests to have your story covered, especially in local news. I have struggled not to put my face on the movement because I thought it took away from the spirit of anonymity. However, the boxes cannot speak for themselves, and I have learned to embrace my role of spokesperson.

Before the Thanksgiving season in 2019, I was contacted about doing an interview and learned afterward that our story was going to be on the cover of the local weekly newspaper. Several months later, we were nominated for Cover Story of the Year, and months after that I was thrilled that the story was chosen for this honor! I was especially pleased that the story itself largely centered around a formerly homeless man that had been helped by our Boxes and was willing to share his story.

I do not know of any other pantry projects that are operating on the scale that ours is here in the Lowcountry. So in the future, I will have my sights set on statewide media and national coverage on the anonymous giving and free pantry movements. Now that projects like mine are more common, I hope to collaborate with other pantry and community refrigerator hosts.

One objective goal that I set for myself (and exceeded) was to have at least ten thousand followers on social media. As I've said, I do not necessarily think that followers on an app translate into action, but every little bit of exposure helps. The more folks who know what we are doing, the more likely we are to get a few of them to become donors to our Boxes, and the more likely we are to find people who need help feeding their families.

Adding a refrigerator to our network of Blessing Boxes was another ambition of mine, especially after the Free Fridge movement started taking over all my social media feeds in 2019. When I found the unit that became our first Free Community Fridge, I was so anxious to get it in place and serving the community that I did not make any changes or improvements to it. Later, I added some stickers and then started sharing photos of it all over the internet. I wish we had recruited artists to make our Free Fridges more visually appealing, but that is another objective on my radar. One of the high schools that hosts a Box has enlisted their art department to decorate the exterior and I have been in touch with an artist via Instagram that is interested in sprucing up another. If the pantries could double as public art spaces, I would feel like we have really achieved something on the next level.

My final goal has been to write a book. Putting everything I have learned into writing is both a way for me to reflect and a way for me to give others a blueprint to recreate what I have done. While I have made it a point to use the word "we" on most of our social media posts, interviews, and email blasts, nearly all the work that went into creating this project has happened at the tips of my fingers on a smart phone. The kindness army that exists now was built by persistent pecking at an iPhone over the course of four years. I have cultivated a motivated group of change-makers, and you can too.

Creating Your Kindness Army

The best advice I can give to anyone considering an endeavor like this is to begin. Wherever you are, however it can be done—just start. You have to start somewhere, and often that first step is a very small one. For me, it was saying the idea out loud to people I trust and listening to their reactions, their concerns, and their questions. Saying your goal aloud forces you to think through your idea and consider the steps you'll need to take to bring it to fruition.

Over the years, I have watched as words I wrote found their way onto the social media pages of other groups doing the same work. I have seen graphics that I made spread over the ocean to pantries and anonymous giving projects in Australia and the UK. I have no idea how many people I have influenced or inspired to participate in anonymous giving in some form.

Some local organizations have declined to be part of our Project—they have built and installed Blessing Boxes but do not, for reasons that are unclear to me, want to be associated with what I have created. It is difficult not to take offense to that, but I remind myself that the point of this work is not to take credit. Kindness is spreading. People are assisting each other not necessarily in a charitable way, but in a way spirited by mutual aid.

There are people who have duplicated this Project already, and I hope there will be more. I hope they keep the anonymity and kindness behind this method of providing food to our neighbors, because in the end, the anonymity is the beauty of it.

I want to reiterate that these Boxes are a small relief on a much larger problem that plagues the food systems in our country, and I hope that in supporting the anonymous giving movement that you will also challenge yourself to learn more about food deserts and food apartheid. We must all work together and support the people and organization that are doing the difficult work to disrupt the systems that only serve the needs of a privileged group. Hunger is a complex problem that necessitates numerous solutions.

Blessing Boxes are not intended to solve the lack of access to fresh, healthy foods for marginalized communities, or any other large-scale food-related issue. Food should not be a privilege. Kids should not be hungry at school. Adults should not have to choose between paying the rent and buying groceries. Find the food activists in your community and support them with your time, your money and your voice.

Thank you for being a part of this movement. Regardless of whether you live near Charleston and donate to the Boxes I have helped create, or you have just learned about the mini-pantry movement and are trying to figure out your next steps, I am grateful for your interest and look forward to seeing what you do with the concept of anonymous giving.

I hope that every time you see a Blessing Box, a Little Free Pantry, or a Free Community Fridge in your neighborhood, you will be reminded that no matter how difficult things may seem—someone in your community cares enough about you to worry if you are going to have enough to eat for dinner tonight.

About the Author

Katie Dahlheim resides in Charleston, South Carolina with her husband and children. She is a graduate of Marshall University and Capital University Law School. Katie has been a practicing attorney since 2007. In 2017, she created the Lowcountry Blessing Box Project, which has inspired countless people to get involved in the battle against food insecurity. There are currently more than 400 anonymous food donation sites in South Carolina. This is her first book.

https://chsblessingbox.org

www.twitter.com/chsblessingbox

www.facebook.com/chsblessingbox

Acknowledgements

It is with gratitude to the earliest supporters of my project that I wish to acknowledge Melody Brown, Renee Vick, Aisha Miller, Kelly Carroll, the Fogle family, Will Kleindienst, Terrylynn Shipley, Jessica Mann, Peggy Lawton and Patty Queen.

Christina Roth and Jessica Hunter, thank you for your guidance and belief in this book.

Luci-Jo DiMaggio, thank you for teaching me to lend a hand.

Thank you to my favorite collaborators: Gretchen Davis, Deborah Powell-Anderson, Tanang Williams, Joy Campbell, Carolyn and Esther Smith, Elizabeth Stribling, Tina Singleton, Germaine Jenkins and Ragina Saunders.

To my people, Kayla Boyter, Stacia Bannerman, Charlene Deter, and Billy Dahlheim: your support made my little idea become a movement.

www.ingramcontent.com/pod-product-compliance
Lightning Source LLC
Chambersburg PA
CBHW062102270326
41931CB00013B/3182